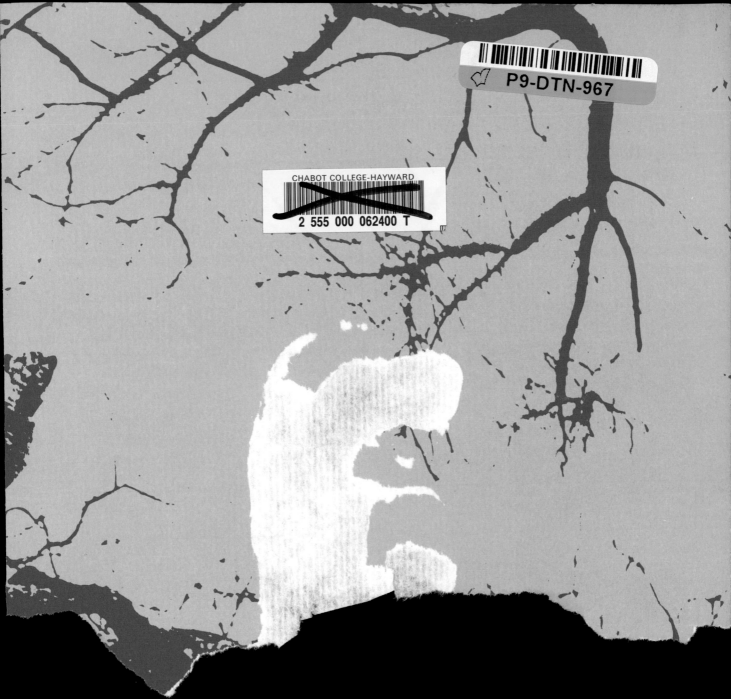

P9-DTN-967

NAN WROGEMANN

Cheetah under the sun

McGraw-Hill Book Company

JOHANNESBURG

DÜSSELDORF LONDON MEXICO MONTREAL NEW YORK
SAO PAULO SYDNEY SINGAPORE TORONTO

ISBN 0 07 091260 2

Set in 11/13 Garamond VIP
Typesetting and design by
Dieter Zimmermann (Pty) Ltd, Johannesburg
Printed and bound by
National Book Printers Ltd., Elsies River, C.P.

"Nothing happens in living Nature that is not in relation to the whole."
– GOETHE

"What has been shaped by man can, if necessary, be shaped again.
An animal that has become extinct is lost forever."
– GUGGISBERG

Contents

Key to Bibliography

To avoid the encumbrance of references within the text, a key to the bibliography appears on page 141. The key refers to page numbers and subject matter and provides the link between the information dealt with in this book and the bibliography on pages 149-156. Information obtained via personal communication is indicated by the abbreviation PC.

Introduction

When McGraw-Hill approached me to edit a series of books on southern African mammals intended for the layman, I welcomed this for a number of reasons. First, while other vertebrates, particularly birds, have enjoyed widespread publicity and as a result are well known, there tends to be a great deal of ignorance about our mammals. Moreover, many of the nocturnal species are unknown to the general public. Second, an increase in knowledge of wildlife tends to stimulate conservation. Third, McGraw-Hill's suggestion that in return for editing the series, a proportion of the author's royalties would be donated to the Mammal Research Institute of Pretoria University, meant that research into our mammals would receive a welcome indirect as well as direct stimulus. It is perhaps significant that this plan should come to fruition during the 10th anniversary of the MRI.

This is the first of an interesting series of books. Not all will cover a single species, some will definitely be about whole groups of mammals. It is perhaps appropriate that the first book in the series should be about an endangered species which has been much in the limelight in recent years due to declining numbers. This informative book brings together all the known facts about the cheetah in a realistic fashion.

The author, Nan Wrogemann, is to be congratulated on her achievement. Not a professional scientist, but somebody who has done intensive research on the cheetah, she has the highest motivation and has shown intense dedication to her task. It was not easy writing a book; she spent several years carrying out research into the literature and writing the manuscript and now her efforts have been crowned by the publication of this magnificent book. We are proud to have her as an Associate Member of the Mammal Research Institute and we hope that she will be encouraged to write more frequently.

J. D. SKINNER

Preface

Late in 1971 I started a survey for the International Union for the Conservation of Nature and the World Wildlife Fund, to assess the status of the cheetah and leopard throughout Africa south of the Sahara. Two years and 2 000-plus interviews later, I know something about the cheetah. I also learned how people in Africa (and in Europe and North America) view the animal. I came to the conclusion that people do not really want the cheetah in this world. A sad story – they want too many competitive things, things that threaten the natural habitat of the cheetah. Those people who believe in reincarnation and would like to have a whirl as an animal next time around, should rather intend returning as cows or housecats or sparrows or rats; they would be better off that way than as wild animals, especially cheetahs.

There are a few bright spots in this dismal scene. There is Mr Atti Port, a rancher to the west of Windhoek, who carries his conservationist convictions to the length of demonstrating to local people that a wild animal need not be dead to be worthy. He tranquilises leopards to enable people to approach the animal, to hold it, to get a close-up feel for the creatures as something other than a devilish perversion of creation. He does this at his own expense. There is Francois Adulla, who is trying to cope, virtually single-handed, with an area of 30 000 square kilometres in the Sahel zone skirting the southern edge of the Sahara. He is trying to resist the adverse impact of climatic desiccation and the resultant biotic degradation and gross overloading of the environment by pastoralist nomads and other starving people. Most dangerous of all for threatened creatures such as the cheetah and addax, are the French mining communities who find a little genteel sport in pursuing desert wildlife with high-speed trucks and high-calibre rifles.

Out of many memorable encounters during the course of travelling over 48 000 kilometres, Nan Wrogemann, wildlife enthusiast, impressed me most. She is a housewife who lives in Randburg, South Africa. Nan recognises that her amateur enthusiasm for wildlife is perhaps limited in terms of "academic rigour", i.e. she realises that she does not know all that there is to know about wild animals. Yet, she recognises that amateur enthusiasm does have a part to play in conservation, and she is determined to make every ounce of her enthusiasm and energy count. She does not, however, recognise how much she is contributing to conservation. Her book, however, speaks for itself. It will lead even the most sceptical to understand what an immense amount a committed citizen can achieve.

I had heard from her before I visited Randburg. She had written to me, asking my advice about a book that she wanted to write about the cheetah. My first reaction was that a number of other housewives in various parts of Africa have written books about wildlife, often about individual creatures (notably orphans), and that they had stirred up extraordinary interest during the 1960's. I wondered, however, if the 1970's did not perhaps need something different to anticipate the problems of the 1980's. I visited Nan Wrogemann at her home, saw what she dismissed as "some preliminary notes" on the topic (files of detailed documentation on every aspect of the cheetah's life history), and reflected how much more material she had collated than many of the recognised experts in the field. Nan's meticulous approach is extraordinary: the least bit of information is traced to remote museum archives in Asia or Europe, and is checked and preferably doublechecked before she is prepared to use it. She then reflects on the theoretical relationships of this piece of information to thousands of other bits of knowledge in her possession. She, certainly more than anyone else I know, tries to have her ideas confirmed or rejected by experts in the professional community. Furthermore, she has a capacity that is not always prominent among the professionals – a creative imagination that provides insight, and which permits the "intuitive leap" across gaps in objective knowledge, to round out a more comprehensive picture of the cheetah.

It is, therefore, a pleasure to write the preface to this book. I hope that it will come into the hands of professionals and amateurs alike: may they all strive to attain the criterion of "conservationist" which Nan Wrogemann holds as her main objective. I suspect that 1980 will see a few more cheetah alive as a consequence of her efforts.

DR NORMAN MYERS

Acknowledgements

It started in Hluhluwe. Four years ago in Zululand, Zululand steeped in history with a new discovery awaiting the receptive visitor around every corner; here it was that my great friend Roger Porter, Regional Scientist at Hluhluwe Game Reserve, first nudged me along the path of this project. During one of our many discussions, this time concerning the cheetah and its precarious situation, Roger said to me, "Now there's a project for you: collect and collate all known literature on cheetah and write a paper." I was startled to say the least, but intrigued. But mainly I thought of the obstacles, undoubtedly insurmountable, which would prevent my carrying through such a project. Still, I discussed it all with my husband, Chris, whose immediate reaction was one of infectious enthusiasm and I was persuaded to visit Professor Waldo Meester, then director of the Mammal Research Institute at Pretoria University, to explain the idea to him and ask his advice. His advice staggered me. "Papers gather dust on shelves," he said, "you'd best write a book for the layman." So this is what I have tried to do.

Professor Meester, who is now professor of zoology at Natal University in Pietermaritzburg, has been of great assistance to me in many ways, reading and criticising parts of the manuscript and making many useful suggestions, especially in the field of taxonomy. Dr Norman Myers has been of immense help, by reading much of my draft work, making numerous suggestions and in general bringing to my attention many little known aspects. Norman also provided me with a number of black and white photographs, for which I am most grateful. He made a great deal of literature available to me, including his field notes used in compiling his status study for I.U.C.N., and his many letters to me were always so full of encouragement. Mr Willie Labuschagne also read much of my draft work and was always ready to assist. He made available to me his list of references to cheetah, which saved me days of work, and during our many discussions together made useful suggestions regarding my general approach to the presentation of the manuscript. He also supplied photographs and gave permission for some of them to be copied as line drawings. Mr Johan Degenaar, who is presently studying the behaviour and reproductive physiology of captive cheetah, also readily supplied me with photographs.

Scientific editing was done by Professor John Skinner, Director of the Mammal Research Institute in Pretoria, who has been extremely helpful. His assistance and advice on many aspects of the manuscript has proved to be of enormous value. His guidance, friendly and straightforward, gave added impetus to the completion of my work.

Leigh Voigt's art work, some of which, such as the different chase postures of cheetah, were drawn from memory after discussions with Willie Labuschagne, delightfully illustrates the physical characteristics of the cheetah. Nola Dingwall undertook the technical line drawings with much enthusiasm and Gerda Pretorius drew the maps. Dr Milton Hildebrand kindly gave permission to use the drawings from his studies of cheetah locomotion and Taylor and Francis of London, publishers of *The Annals and Magazine of Natural History*, gave permission to reproduce the drawings by Mr R. I. Pocock. Weidenfeld and Nicolson gave permission to reproduce the drawing of the Giant Cheetah from the book *Pleistocene Mammals of Europe* by B. Kurtén. The drawings by R. Broom are reproduced with kind permission of the Transvaal Museum in Pretoria.

Dr C. K. Brain, director of the Transvaal Museum, allowed me the use of a photograph and, whenever I wanted to, let me work in the Museum Library. Mrs de Kok (who has since left) and Miss Maryna Oberholzer both of the library staff must be thanked for tracking down many references for me. Nico Dippenaar, also of the Museum, helped with references to taxonomy.

Dr Reay Smithers, director of The National Museums and Monuments of Rhodesia in Salisbury, has been particularly helpful with information on the king cheetah. His letters to me helped to sort out a lot of confusion which surrounded the king cheetah skins. Miss Daphne Hills, zoologist at the British Museum (Natural History) in London supplied me with information on king cheetah skins and Sir Archibald James of England very kindly sent me information on the king cheetah as well.

I relied very heavily on comments and suggestions from a number of other people. At the Kruger National Park, Dr U. de V. Pienaar, Director of Nature Conservation at Skukuza, has indeed been most helpful. Dr Eddie Young, formerly of the Division of Veterinary Services at Skukuza and Mr S. C. L. Joubert were also of help. Dr V. de Vos, now head of the Veterinary Services, assisted with my list on parasites and chemical immobilisation, and made many useful suggestions. Others have also assisted me in several directions: Professor Fritz Eloff, Dr W. von Richter, Dr George Schaller, Dr George Frost, Dr H. Ebedes, Dr Eugene Joubert, Mr James Clarke, Dr Dave Meltzer, Dr Oluf Martiny, Dr Peter Becker, Miss Creina Bond, Mr Ted Davison, Mr N. A. Ferreira, Mr George Frame, Dr Hans Heinz, Mr Peter Jackson, Dr J. Pringle, Mr Chris Stuart, Mr Bert Woodhouse, Mr J. H. Oosthuizen and Mr C. J. Rocher. The director and staff of Aloe Book Agency, Mr Lionel Schroder, Mrs Botha and Mrs Buist were very co-operative in obtaining literature for me.

Rather extensive correspondence between myself and various zoos and safari parks where cheetah have been bred enabled me to update my list of captive births: Mr V. J. A. Manton of Whipsnade Park, England; Mr Lawrence Curtis and Mr V. Camp of the Oklahoma City Zoo, U.S.A.; Mr Bill York (formerly of Lion Country Safari in the U.S.A.); Mr Pat Quinn of Lion Country Safari; Dr Charles Vallat of Montpellier Zoo, France; Mr Julian Tong of the Beekse Bergen Park in Holland, and of course in South Africa, Mr John Spence of High Noon Game Farm in the Cape Province. I would particularly like to thank Dr Bedford Vestal, Research Scientist at the Oklahoma City Zoo in America, who readily made available to me records of captive births of cheetah.

A special word of thanks to Ann and Godfrey van Dyk of De Wildt Estates for their kind hospitality. A Cheetah Research Centre was established by Dr D. J. Brand, Director of the Pretoria Zoological Gardens, at the De Wildt Estates farm in 1971. I was able to visit Ann and Godfrey on many occasions and to observe, at close proximity, the cheetah there. This was pure delight for me, and I feel most grateful that I had these opportunities.

It would be sadly remiss of me not to mention the role my family played whilst I was engaged in the research and writing of this book. My husband assisted me in many ways. Not only did he constantly cajole and urge me onwards when my spirits were flagging, but he shared my enthusiasm right from the beginning. Together we spent long hours discussing the literature and the views, so often apparently anomalous, expressed by the various writers. He also read and copy-edited the manuscript, and helped me when it came to equations and figure work. Our two children, Trevor (who suggested the title of my book) and Gail, helped out at home when mother was glued to the typewriter. My mother, Mrs Stella Wright, readily took over domestic duties when I was away and my sister-in-law, Mrs Linda Wright, spent many hours typing out draft work.

I owe a lot to my publishers; in particular I am most grateful to Mr Rolf Pakendorf for his guidance and advice.

Finally, a word about the book itself. This is not the result of a field study nor a study of cheetah in any one particular area. To me, after a great deal of reading and research into available literature relating to cheetah, there seemed to be a distinct lack of knowledge on a number of aspects. I felt compelled to find out so many things, to write them down, and from what we do know about this creature, to present as clear a picture as possible, how it lives, what it eats, how much it eats, and, in general, its life style. Gradually, piece by piece, I fitted my "cheetah puzzle" together. But there are gaps in the puzzle which I cannot fill, and I sincerely hope that this book will prove a stimulus for future study.

Photograph Acknowledgements

(BLACK AND WHITE)

Dr C.K. Brain, no. 20

Johan Degenaar, nos. 1, 2, 5, 6, 13, 14, 23, 24

Willie Labuschagne, nos. 7, 8, 9, 10, 18, 19, 21

Norman Myers, nos. 11, 12, 15, 16, 17, 22, 28, 29, 30, 31, 32, 33

National Museums & Monuments of Rhodesia, nos. 3, 4

Ann van Dyk, nos. 25, 26, 27

(COLOUR)

Gary Schoof, king cheetah.

Willie Labuschagne, cheetah about to leap forward; cheetah threatens photographer; threat posture; black cub in the Kalahari.

Johan Degenaar, cheetah bares its teeth; mating posture; close up of mating posture showing neck bite; captive female which produced five cubs (Collisheen Estates, Natal).

Photographs used on the dust jacket and inside covers by kind permission of Willie Labuschagne.

1 Profile

The cheetah derives its special fascination for man from its legendary swiftness. Sleek and nimble, a cheetah on the hunt is a truly remarkable sight. Its fleetness of foot is a feature not only of the modern day cheetah, for fossil records show clearly that in the past the Giant Cheetah, *Acinonyx pardinensis,* which roamed Europe during the Villafranchian (1,9 to 3,8 million years ago), was the size of a lion and could run as fast as the present day cheetah. The giant cheetah was fairly common then, and its "slender bones and typical teeth" are found at Pardines, Villaroya, Senèze, Olivola and other Villafranchian sites. What a magnificent spectacle this creature must have been in those bygone days.

Cheetah, the name is derived from the Hindu word "chita" meaning "spotted one", did not confine its domain to Europe, its range during the Lower Pleistocene (refer to the geological time chart on page 4) extended as far as India and China. Through the ages both its range and its size decreased so that by the Middle Pleistocene a transition to a smaller form, *Acinonyx intermedius,* had taken place. By the Upper Pleistocene, the resemblance to the present day animal was close enough for it to have been classified as *Acinonyx jubatus.*

But the cheetah's evolutionary history goes back even further than the Lower Pleistocene. Cheetah were a distinct species in the late Pliocene and the existence of cheetah fossils from the Pliocene of India has been recorded. The emergence of cheetah as a distinct cat predator even during the mid-Miocene seems a possibility as the African Felidae were established, well-defined carnivores at that time. This could indicate that cheetah originated in Africa, and that they appeared some 18 to 20 million years ago. It is perhaps significant that cheetah may have emerged as a distinct species at a time in our evolutionary history when grasslands were rapidly spreading and taking over forests, and the gazelles, a suitable prey animal for the cheetah, became prominent. A complementary arrangement whereby predator and prey evolved simultaneously.

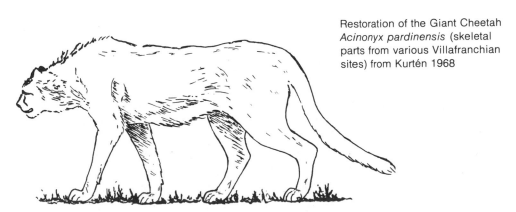

Restoration of the Giant Cheetah *Acinonyx pardinensis* (skeletal parts from various Villafranchian sites) from Kurtén 1968

It is evident that cheetah have inhabited this planet for a very long while. Longer probably than lion and leopard, which became distinctive predators in the Lower Pleistocene. But the history of cheetah suggests that although they inhabited a wide range of territory, they were never abundant in number. And the trend today is towards even fewer cheetah due to the steady, and in some areas, rapid elimination of habitat tolerable to this species. Much of the total range of the cheetah has been swamped by livestock, since man and his cattle prefer the grassland vegetation, the type of habitat where cheetah would usually have been found. Agricultural development and new settlements, punctuating the once vast open areas, have played havoc with cheetah habitat in East Africa, as with most other areas. I contemplate the future of cheetah with mounting apprehension.

The leopard has been able to hold out under these circumstances far more ably than has the cheetah. Generally, man does not disturb forest areas for agriculture and livestock grazing when other more attractive alternatives are available, and the leopard in many areas can, and does, live side by side with man, sometimes unknown to him. Only a few hours drive from Johannesburg in the Transvaal province in South Africa, are areas where the odd wild leopard may still be found. But not cheetah. This animal is too sensitive to man's depredations to the already delicately balanced environment. Cheetah are subject to direct and indirect pressures from all quarters, but loss of habitat is the most critical. This is not to say that other factors, such as the fur trade, elimination of prey species and competition from other carnivores, especially hyaena, do not represent a threat to this animal's survival. Protection of any species is no easy matter and because cheetah are sparsely distributed the protection of this animal is made all the more difficult.

Myers cites a figure of ten to fifteen thousand cheetah living in Africa, south of the Sahara. This may give the impression that there are lots of cheetah about, and that we need not concern ourselves over the status of this species for some time yet. But these numbers are estimates and Myers indicates that they could be out by as much as 50%. So let us consider the *trend* in cheetah population numbers, rather than the total. About ten years ago there were something like twice as many cheetah as there are today. And unless immediate and stringent conservation measures are taken, this rate of decline will continue, and possibly even accelerate in the future. The animal has nowhere to go. It is being pushed out of its natural habitat, and in many cases forced onto farms and ranches. Hence some reports that cheetah numbers are increasing whereas they are only becoming more prominent in areas which they previously avoided. And man's utilisation of the land increases. And the human population increases. And the livestock increases. Where *can* the cheetah go?

If we look at a map of Africa, and write in the various estimates of cheetah numbers for each country within the continent, we see that the total is made up mainly of small "pocket" populations. There are some exceptions, mainly in South West Africa, Botswana and in the countries of East Africa. For the rest we read estimates such as 50 cheetah living in Malawi, 400 and less in Rhodesia (with an anticipated drop to 200 and less by 1980), 200 in Mocambique, and so

1

2

1 Lithe and graceful even
when walking
2 The facial markings of
each cheetah are unique
and can be used as a
means of identification

on. These pocket populations simply cannot hold out for any great length of time against all those factors militating against their survival. Such small populations are very easily overcome by the adverse environmental conditions into which they are forced through the exploitation by man of their natural habitat. But another threat confronts the cheetah. Prey animals, because of heavy poaching, are decreasing at an alarming rate and in some areas have completely disappeared. This is especially so of the countries in West Africa bordering the Sahara Desert. Due to the severe climatic conditions, the nomadic pastoralists face continual difficulties in the Sahel belt which borders the southern Sahara. The vast Sahel, stretching across Africa from the Atlantic Ocean to the Red Sea, has become a land of desolate devastation. Even under favourable conditions this area is hot and dry, but after five years of drought and sad pastoral mismanagement, parts of the desert advance several kilometres

Geological time chart (not to scale) showing possible evolutionary history of the cheetah

PLEISTOCENE	Upper 200 000	Cat-predators widespread in Africa, India and southwestern Asia; CHEETAH REDUCED IN SIZE TO BE CLASSED AS *ACINONYX JUBATUS;* RANGED IN CHINA AND INDIA; BECAME EXTINCT IN EASTERN ASIA AT CLOSE OF THE ICE AGE
	Middle *1,1	CHEETAH, A SMALLER FORM *(ACINONYX INTERMEDIUS)* RANGED AS FAR EAST AS CHINA; sabre-tooth cats declining; hyaena less numerous
	Lower *3,5	Possible emergence of the big cats, the lion, leopard, tiger, etc., as distinctive species; THE GIANT CHEETAH *(ACINONYX PARDINENSIS)* ROAMED EUROPE, INDIA, CHINA; hyaena and sabre-tooth cats numerous
CENOZOIC ("recent life")	*3,75 Pliocene *7,5	CHEETAH A DISTINCTIVE SPECIES; hyaena numerous
	Miocene *26	Sabre-tooth cats emerge; possible emergence of hyaena (an aberrant form); POSSIBLE EMERGENCE IN AFRICA OF CHEETAH; gazelle become more prominent
	Oligocene *40	Forerunners of the felids and canids emerge; grasseaters spread rapidly as grasslands take over forests
	Eocene *60	Family Miacidae of the order *Creodonta* develops – accepted as the ancestor of our modern day carnivores
	Paleocene *70	

4

* = million years

each year. What sparse vegetation remains is fast disappearing and even the human population can no longer exist without foreign assistance. The West African countries are in dire straits and there is little chance of the existing cheetah populations surviving for more than just a few years.

Yet a spark of hope persists. Cheetah, it seems, can recover from a relatively small gene pool. In Iran some ten to fifteen years ago, cheetah numbered about one hundred, but there are now said to be about two hundred and possibly more. This increase is due to the authorities having encouraged the recovery of the prey species such as gazelle and wild sheep by the introduction of legislation to cut down on poaching. In Natal (South Africa) in 1965, 64 cheetah were introduced into the local game reserves, and today there are about 110. A small and slow growth, but nevertheless this demonstrates that cheetah can survive, and even increase, under favourable conditions.

Cheetah have long been associated with man, but their history is one of decline. Time is running out for this cat. If we are prepared to face and tackle the problems, to concede to the cheetah its place in the sun, we may yet save from extinction this creature so regal and aloof, so beautiful and lithe, in movement a symphony of natural grace.

2 Cheetah and Man

The cheetah . . .

The cheetah is a cat, in spite of the doubts and opinions to the contrary. Way back in 1776 Schreber classed this animal under the cat family, *Felis.* Many features of its physical appearance attest to its feline lineage, the slightly rounded face, large eyes and well developed earflaps with their comparatively high partition are the most apparent. Physiological evidence is also available; for example, cheetah have a diploid chromosome count of 38, a characteristic of all but two of the members of the family Felidae. There are a number of differences in the anatomy of cheetah distinguishing it from the other cats which led to its being accorded its own separate genus, *Acinonyx,* created by Brookes in 1828. The most striking contrast concerns the cheetah's claws, which, when retracted are not covered by a protective sheath. This tends to give the misleading impression that the cheetah cannot retract its claws at all. The claws are thus fully visible at all times and the "dog-like" appearance of a cheetah's

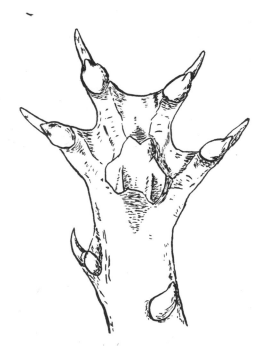

Lower view of extended left forepaw of cheetah with hairs cut short to show the extent of the interdigital webs and the complete absence of integumental claw-sheaths

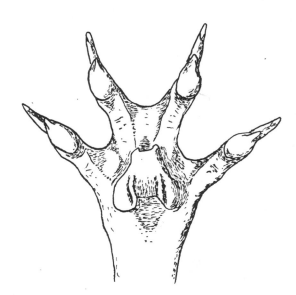

The same of the left hind paw
(from Pocock 1916)

foot has led to some confusion, many people still believing that the cheetah is "somewhere between a cat and a dog". The high, almost bony haunches, and the dome shape of its head add further to the differences between this animal and other big cats. There are differences within the skull as well. The jaws of a cheetah are smaller, and the canines less developed than those of the big cats, the lion, tiger, leopard, snow leopard and jaguar, and the skull takes on a brittle and fragile appearance when compared to that of a lion.

But there is another important difference which sets this animal apart from the larger cats. The larynx, which is the upper part of the windpipe, is connected to the skull by means of a number of small hyoid bones. In the large cats, but not in cheetah, these hyoid bones are separated by strong elastic ligaments which provide a "sounding board" and enable them to roar, whilst the cheetah's vocalization is confined to sounds such as a purr and a chirp, the latter very much like the call of a bird. Once you have heard a cheetah purr, which it does just like a domestic cat but with greater volume, then you cannot doubt that the cheetah is a cat. Richard Owen, in a dissertation on the anatomy of cheetah dating back to 1835, was probably the first person to point out this difference in the hyoid equipment of the cats.

Over the ages, cheetah and the other cats have sacrificed some of their chewing teeth, and to compensate for this, have developed digestive systems which can deal with huge chunks of meat. The jaws lack mobility and the lower jaw cannot move sideways in the manner of grass eating animals. Instead, cheetah possess a powerful masseter muscle which moves the jaw up and down and provides the vice-like strength for gripping a prey animal. The tongue, well adapted for licking, is covered with an arrangement of papillae, horny projections which make this organ extremely rough. Adult cheetah have a total

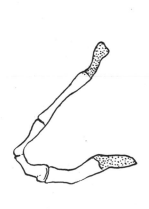

Lateral view of hyoid of cheetah, showing the structure of this apparatus; and

lateral view of hyoid of leopard (from Pocock 1916)

of thirty teeth (the cubs have twenty-six), sixteen upper and fourteen lower, ten less than their primitive relatives, the Viverridae, which include civet, genet and mongoose, and fourteen less than their ancestors, the Miacidae. Fewer teeth do not appear to be a handicap though for the cheetah's digestive system and the development of the carnassials compensate for this loss. The carnassials, teeth which evolved from upper and lower pre-molars, work in scissor like fashion enabling the animal to grip and tear flesh. Notice how a cheetah uses these "cheek teeth" by holding its head at a sideways angle when eating.

The pelage (fur) of cheetah does not vary dramatically throughout its present range but, to some degree, the shade of the ground colour and the diameter and arrangements of the black spots differ from one animal to another. In some, the ground colour may be a light to pale ochre while other animals have a darker tawny shade which, particularly in the sunlight, looks a mellow golden colour. Some animals have a slightly darker strip of colouring along the dorsal area, but this usually occurs when the ground colour itself is rather dark. The fur is not very long, even on the shoulders, and the mane is short. The hairs of the mane are erect, in contrast to the rest of the pelage which is mostly smooth and trim. However, under conditions where temperatures drop below freezing cheetah have been known to grow a "dense and luxurious" fur as recorded from the Zoological Park in Ontario. The limbs and feet are generally spotted, although in one sub-species, *soemmeringii,* described by Fitzinger in 1855, an absence of spots on the hind feet was noted.

The black spots of the pelage may vary from 1¼ to 2 cm across. The larger and therefore more prominent black spots are interspersed with much smaller and sometimes indistinct black spots, the intensity of which also varies. The larger spots may be closely or irregularly placed. The belly of a cheetah is not

8   Profile, showing short snout   Full face, showing roundness and characteristic tear line

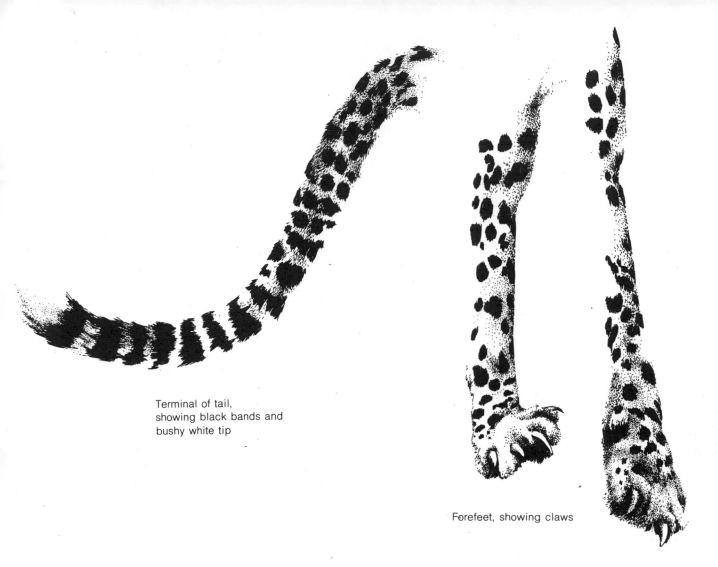

Terminal of tail,
showing black bands and
bushy white tip

Forefeet, showing claws

spotted. The black tear line, unique to cheetah, extends from the eye to the upper lip on each side of the face. The purpose of this tear line is not immediately clear, but Eaton suggests that it cuts down the glare from the sun. The tail is spotted and is about half the length of the rest of the animal. The end of the tail is not spotted and instead there are about four to six black bands, some more perfectly formed than others, and the tip of the tail is white and bushy. Both the adult male and the female are similarly marked, and it is no simple matter to tell males and females apart, except with an experienced eye. Males are generally slightly larger than females and they may have a thicker neck but there are no outstanding features to indicate the sex, whereas lions, as opposed to lionesses, are described by Schaller as "moving haystacks" because of their manes. Who knows why the appearance of males and females of some species of mammals are so different and others alike? Another of Nature's mysteries.

There appears to be a fair amount of division of opinion regarding sub-species of cheetah. Some authors recognise five or six sub-species throughout the present range while others don't recognise any sub-species at all. Everyone is entitled to their own opinion but I do feel that this subject is best dealt with by the specialists qualified in that particular field of systematics. I have used the *Preliminary Identification Manual for African Mammals* for this purpose and acknowledge five sub-species, as listed in Appendix I. The differences from one sub-species to another are very subtle so that one cannot make easy distinctions as to the characteristics and appearance of each. There are, and always will be, variations within a sub-species. I recall two cheetah from the same litter which I saw at De Wildt Estates. The one, a female, has a dark tawny ground colour, and small (I guess about 1½ cm in diameter) closely arranged black spots. Her brother has a much lighter ground colour, spots larger and not as closely arranged. The difference in the markings of these two litter mates from the Transvaal in South Africa is very striking.

Variations in the markings and appearance of these animals have been recorded in a number of instances. The king cheetah, an aberrant form of the common cheetah, has most unusual markings and is discussed in a separate chapter. Another unusually marked cheetah was recorded from the Beaufort West district in the Cape Province in 1877, and given the name *Felis lanea* by Sclater. A description of this animal, a male and not fully grown, is quoted from the *Proceedings of the Zoological Society, London:*

"It presents generally the appearance of a Cheetah (*Felis jubata*) but is thicker in the body, and has shorter and stouter limbs, and a much thicker tail. When adult it will probably be considerably larger than the Cheetah, and is larger even now than our three specimens of that animal. The fur is much more wooly and dense than in the Cheetah, as is particularly noticeable on the ears, mane and tail. The whole of the body is of a pale isabelline colour, rather paler on the belly and lower parts, but covered all over, including the belly, with roundish dark fulvous blotches. There are no traces of the black spots which are so conspicuous in all the varieties of the Cheetah which I have seen, nor of the characteristic black line between the mouth and eye."

This was most probably a form of albinism of which about three records from this same district exist. From India comes another record of albinism in which the spots, normally black, were of a blue colour, and the whiteness of the ground colour showed a bluish tendency. A young cheetah which was killed in Northern Rhodesia, now Zambia, in the 1930's was also found to have an unusual skin. The whole of the dorsal area was covered from the head to the tip of the tail by a continuous mat of long hairs. The colour of the pelage was a dirty-whitish grey, which was faintly streaked with darker grey. The skin was profusely covered with black spots and the usual tawny ground colour present in cheetah was only apparent on the face, the fore-legs and the hind-legs below the hocks. The tail was mainly black.

Of the members of the family Felidae, the caracal is one species in which the structure of the hind feet resembles that of a cheetah. The caracal, as well as the cheetah, was used in India to hunt game, and large numbers of these animals were kept and trained for this purpose.

... and Man

"Oh, great king, do not be angry, you will kill the next one," chanted the keeper of the cheetah. The silent crowd moved aside as the keeper led the cheetah back to its cart.

A scene typical of the many such incidents that must have taken place in 17th century India, where cheetah were kept for the purpose of hunting black buck. This cheetah had been unsuccessful in bringing down a buck, but it was still treated with the utmost respect. The coursing of cheetah was a popular sport, and Akbar the Great, the Moghul emperor who ruled over Hindustan from 1556 to 1605 was extremely fond of cheetah, as were the other Moghul emperors, and it is recorded that Akbar kept some 1 000 cheetah for the purpose of hunting black buck. Cheetah were held in high esteem, and hundreds of people would congregate to watch the long-legged animal sprint after its prey. A successful kill brought about much applause and jubilation and the cheetah was always rewarded with a cup of warm blood from the victim. During one hunting expedition in India, a cheetah and a deer it was pursuing each performed a leap of unbelievable length. In the path of the prey animal was a ravine some 23 metres across, which the deer cleared. It is recorded that the cheetah, "in its eagerness", took itself over the ravine and seized the deer. The spectators, beholding this amazing feat, rejoiced, and the cheetah was raised in rank to chief of the cheetahs. Further, as a special honour, it was ordered that a drum be beaten in front of this animal.

Cheetah were used by the Arabs and Abyssinians to hunt antelope, and by the end of the 16th century, trained cheetah were a fairly common sight at hunting lodges in Africa. This sport rapidly spread as far as Italy, where the animal was again associated with aristocracy. The sport of coursing is well known to many. Usually adult cheetah were used in the taming and training process as they were the most successful in the hunts. A hood was placed over the cheetah's head and the animal conveyed by cart close to a herd of black buck. The hood was then removed and on seeing the prey animals the cheetah would streak after them. An extremely striking and, I think, unique painting by George Stubbs depicts two keepers with a tamed cheetah harnessed and ready for a hunt.

Kublai Khan, the fifth of the great Mongol khans, was often accompanied on riding expeditions by cheetah. The Mongols had trained cheetah to run down antelope and fallow deer. Marco Polo, who spent many years in the Khan's civil service, on his return to Europe brought back numerous tales of the zoological gardens and game reserves of the Kublai Khan, and described an animal that he had seen as a long-legged "leopard", referring of course to cheetah. The 15th century saw the cheetah indeed treated as a royal subject. Marie of Burgundy, who had her own small zoo, wanted a cheetah. And so, in fitting style, a cheetah crossed Mt Cenia in mid-winter on the rump of a horse, muffled up in a cape. Francis I, who reigned as king of France for 32 years during the 16th century, was so fond of animals, that he would take them with him on his travels. Cheetah were included, and it is said that he played with them as if they were pet poodles.

But the cheetahs' association with man goes back further in our history than the 16th century. The ancient Egyptians regarded the cheetah as a sacred animal, and the pharaohs believed that after death their spirits would be carried away on the backs of these fleet-footed animals. Cheetah were trained for hunting, and this is portrayed in many sculptured decorations in the tombs of the pharaohs. Found in Tutankhamen's tomb was a "magnificent statuette of the king placed on a walking cheetah". Tutankhamen, the youngest of the pharaohs, came to the throne at the age of nine, and died after ruling for only nine years. When his tomb was discovered in 1922 by Howard Carter, many objects were found representing cheetah. A beautifully painted box, which contained the young king's sandals, had attached to it a wooden carving in the form of a cheetah head. A triangular chest within the tomb, on which was depicted a hunting scene, was flanked on each end by a finely sculpted cheetah's head. There were three funerary couches, each in the shape of an animal, and each was to serve the spirit of the young king in some manner. One of these couches discovered in the antechamber of the tomb takes the shape of a cheetah, made of stuccoed and gilded wood. The animal's eyes are of crystal and the characteristic tear line and the muzzle are enhanced with an outline of blue glass-paste. The protective cheetah "vigilantly guarded the pharaoh throughout his reconstructed reign", writes Desroches-Noblecourt in her fascinating account on the life and death of the young pharaoh.

In Southern Africa cheetah do not appear to have played any major role relative to man in the early days. The bushmen who, in times gone by, inhabited most of Southern Africa left behind them a wealth of rock art, engravings and paintings. Their subject matter was mainly drawn from situations which affected them in their daily routine, and nowhere in the numerous rock paintings in South Africa now left to posterity is a cheetah portrayed. Most animals which crossed their paths were used as art subjects, and of ostrich there exist numerous fine engravings, and eland feature prominently in rock paintings. The abundance of the depictions of ostrich indicates, of course, that this large bird played a meaningful role in their lives. The bushmen collected ostrich eggs and used the shells for carrying water on their nomadic travels. The eland was doubtless a source of food. Various scenes were reproduced with great astuteness, often having as subject matter antelope and ritualistic dancing, with some of these diminutive peoples themselves portrayed as animals. But the cheetah was not reproduced, and felines generally were not a popular subject for rock art, probably because they did not constitute a major food item. Dr Hans Heinz, an authority on the Kalahari bushmen, informs me that although bushmen eat the flesh of cheetah, this is probably not a "regular" source of meat supply. Apparently, the bushmen still surviving do eat the flesh from cheetah, but to what extent this happens is not easily gauged.

There does exist, in the Matopos in Rhodesia, an unusual rock frieze which depicts twelve cheetah at play. Bert Woodhouse, an authority on rock art, says that this frieze was the work of the Later Stone Age People, and although no rock paintings have been accurately dated, it is reasonable to suppose that this frieze is between 1 000 and 2 000 years old.

Most of the tribes of Southern Africa use the skins of animals for various ceremonial purposes, and here again the cheetah features very little, if at all. The chief of any tribe is usually adorned with a leopard skin during ceremonies, but Dr Peter Becker, a world authority on African customs, beliefs and history, has told me that if a complete leopard skin is unobtainable, or if only a small portion of a leopard skin is available, a combination of the skins of leopard and cheetah will be used. But this only happens if the tribe is not all that particular about detail. It is the spots on an animal skin that are of significance, a tradition dating back to the time of Shaka in the 19th century. However, the exact significance of the spots is not clear (relating perhaps to bravery or dignity) but even in Johannesburg today if a ceremony is planned, Africans will buy skins from curio shops, demanding first leopard, which they sometimes call "tiger", then, if this is not available, cheetah. One local dealer told me she even sells ocelot skins; the skin just has to be spotted.

David Livingstone, adventurer of the dark African continent, related that the Bakalahari, supposedly the oldest of the Bechuana tribes, often bartered the skins of animals in exchange for knives, tobacco and various other supplies. Some of the skins were worn by the local inhabitants, but a large proportion were made up into karosses and sold to traders. But one should mention that the early tribes did not attach great importance to these skins per se, in contrast to the traders, who found them highly desirable. Of course, the demand raised the value of the skins in the eyes of these tribes and they soon learned that worthwhile payment was obtainable if such skins were made available to the traders. Divinatory bones, used by witchdoctors, are obtained from a wide variety of animals, and divinatory sets and techniques vary from tribe to tribe. Each object in the set represents a person, a thing or a mood either past, present or future. For instance, the bones of a leopard, "the cunning hunter", would represent "dignity, regality, prosperity, longevity", says Peter Becker. Occasionally the phalanges (bones of the foot) of a cheetah, representing "fleet-footedness", are included in a set of divinatory bones.

Today cheetah and man are still associated, but the relationship ranges from admiration and attempts at conservation to an extreme of cold blooded near genocide. Perhaps genocide is not quite the right word but I hope it gets the message over. Because this is what is happening. Snared and shot, no effort is spared to provide skins for the worshippers of high fashion. In Johannesburg alone the trade in cheetah skins is enormous. I spent some time in 1971 conducting a survey of the trade in these skins, and what I discovered appalled me. The trade is brisk and active, and nearly every curio dealer or furrier I approached made it clear that a customer could always be assured of getting a skin. "There's no need to worry about getting a skin, our stocks never run out", was one comment. "We have a steady influx of these skins", was yet another reply. Some of the smaller shops did not have any cheetah skins available when I visited them "because they are very scarce". But one shop owner did add that if I contacted him again in a month's time he would have a few cheetah skins in stock. On sale at one shop were "jaunty little jackets", made from the skins of cheetah cubs.

Once revered and held in great esteem, these rare animals are now destroyed for the sake of fashion. What an incredible change in attitude.

A fur dealer in Johannesburg made a statement in a local newspaper in 1973 to the effect that at least 1 000 cheetah and leopard skins are processed every three months in Johannesburg. The dealer himself handles about 400-600 spotted skins a year, half of which are cheetah skins. Mr James Clarke, assistant to the editor of one of the daily newspapers in the Transvaal, who did a snap survey in 1973 on the trade in cheetah skins, wrote at the time: "I have no reason to disbelieve his figures – his shop was full of spotted skins." There have been some attempts by furriers to end the trade in spotted cat skins, and in fact in about 1970, a few Johannesburg furriers vowed never to deal with spotted furs again. One furrier's words, as reported in a newspaper, were: ". . . it is a voluntary, independent decision of conscience following exhaustive research". Today, the sentiments of this same furrier have changed, because, as he said, his livelihood was being threatened. He felt that he could no longer afford to lose sales of leopard skins, ". . . although I have definite proof that continued sales means the extinction of the animal".

Where do all these skins come from? And where do they go?

Most of the dealers I approached said the skins came from Rhodesia, Botswana, South West Africa and "a few" from the Transvaal and Mocambique. There is obviously an active border-spanning trade going on, and I remain firm in my belief that Johannesburg serves as a central clearing depot for skins from the countries mentioned. These skins are destined for the international market, and Myers writes that officials in every country in Africa and South America he visited during his survey period stated, that if the demand were to be reduced, they would be able to enforce what legislation they have. In 1968 and 1969 something like 3 168 cheetah skins were imported into the United States, but since protective legislation was passed in 1972, prohibiting the import of any spotted cat skins, sales have dropped. Unfortunately, there remain one or two shops where, for a few hundred extra dollars, a spotted fur coat is sold from "under the counter". Banning the sale of spotted skins in one country, however, leads to a shift in trade to another country, and Myers comments that there are signs that Japan is now entering the market.

In South Africa, there is no law which prohibits the import of these spotted cat skins, although the Fur Association does attempt to ensure that only skins obtained legitimately (via culling in game reserves or from animals shot under licence), are imported into this country. Herein lies the problem. Without legislation in South Africa, neighbouring countries, such as Botswana, who do have protective legislation, find their laws difficult to enforce, bordering as they do, a country where these animals are termed "vermin" and no veterinary permit is required for carnivore skins. The possessor of a skin has no obligation to obtain a permit of origin. The claim that 1 000 cheetah and leopard skins are processed in Johannesburg every three months indicates that skins are being obtained not only by legitimate means. I cannot accept that such a high number of cheetah and leopard are culled or shot under licence – every three months. It was reported in a newspaper in Johannesburg that most of the skins dealt with by a particular trader originated from Botswana, and yet the Botswana authorities had not issued a permit for a cheetah skin during the two years prior to the report. It is obviously very difficult to enforce any sort of legislation in one country unless all neighbouring countries establish import and export regulations for these skins.

There are, of course, genuine cases where a farmer, whose livestock is threatened by a marauding predator, has to shoot. He is in fact licensed to do so. The farmer, we must be prepared to acknowledge, has to protect his interests. But very often the shoooting of a predator is indiscriminate and irresponsible. I have it on reliable authority that in South West Africa several dozen cheetah were shot on two farmlands over a period of one year. One wonders whether these animals were genuine "marauders" or merely the victims of man's hunting instinct.

The Mammal Research Institute in Pretoria has instigated an intensive and thorough survey into the fur trade, which, says Professor John Skinner, Director of the Institute, will hopefully clarify the situation. Steps have been taken by some authorities in an endeavour to control, and ultimately stop, the sale of spotted cat skins. In October 1971, the Kruger National Park authorities announced that they had banned the sale of cheetah and leopard skins, and articles made from them, within their reserves. The Parks Board in Natal followed suit. Dr Pienaar, Director for Nature Conservation at the Kruger National Park said at the time of the banning that he would like to see a general boycott of cheetah and leopard skins and any products derived from them. "This will reduce the demand and cut down on the hunting of leopard and cheetah," he said.

Man has become an irresponsible predator, an ominous sign of the times.

3 The King Cheetah

Few animals have caused such widespread interest, stretching over a number of decades, as has the aberrant form of the common cheetah, known as the king cheetah. The interest continues to this day, and quite surprisingly, in spite of numerous sightings of this animal no one had succeeded in taking a photograph of a live king cheetah until very recently. In the November 1974 issue of *Custos,* the National Parks Board of South Africa publication, a photograph of a king cheetah taken by Mr Gary Schoof in the Kruger National Park has been reproduced. To my knowledge, this photograph is unique. The king cheetah is characterised by its unusual markings, which on its dorsal area are radically different from those of a normal cheetah, and give this animal a splendidly regal appearance. Instead of the usual round black spots, the markings are broad longitudinal black stripes. The spots on the side of the pelage and on the legs meld to form irregularly shaped blotches and bands. It is not uncommon for members of the Felidae to produce aberrant forms, and after examining photographs of three skins of king cheetah, I noticed that although the markings were similar, each had its own individual pattern, making these unusual felid skins quite distinct from one another.

In Rhodesia in 1926, the skin of a king cheetah was discovered by Major A.L. Cooper, who said at the time that the animal, although not identified, was most probably known for some twenty years before this discovery which, he said, was borne out by the fact that "mention used to be made round camp fires by natives, of a beast that was neither lion, leopard nor cheetah". King cheetah were apparently not all that rare early in this century, and Mr Jackson, an Assistant Native Commissioner in Rhodesia wrote at the time that "many years ago these animals were fairly common". At the time of Major Cooper's discovery, the possibility of this animal being a hybrid between a leopard and a cheetah was raised, but Cooper dismissed this supposition as unlikely. This animal was considered by some to be a mythical creature and was also referred to as the Mazoe leopard, Mazoe being a town situated to the north of Salisbury, Rhodesia.

Major Cooper was first shown the skin by Sir Clarkson Tredgold, then Chief Justice of Rhodesia and chairman of the Queen Victoria Memorial Library and Museum Committee, from whom he learned that it had been presented to the Salisbury Museum by Mr Donald Fraser, who had purchased the skin from "natives". The natives informed Mr Fraser that they had killed this animal in the Macheke District, (now the Marandellas area in Rhodesia) and that it was one of four or five animals of a group. It is not clear whether the animal that was killed was one of a group of king cheetah, or if the others in the group were common cheetah. This point is particularly interesting since in 1935 Mr D. Townley, who lived near Birchenough Bridge in Rhodesia, bought a king cheetah skin from natives who killed this animal on the north bank of the Lower Sabi river. This king cheetah was in a group of three other cheetah, all of which were the common cheetah.

Major Cooper's first thought when he examined the skin taken from the Macheke District was that it was unlike any animal he knew, and he described it as being similar to the leopard in build, judging from the skin, and being "heavier and more stockily built than a cheetah, yet there were the distinct, non-retractile (sic) claws of this animal". He was convinced that he had discovered a new species of cheetah, and sent photographs of this skin to Mr Oldfield Thomas, a well-known zoologist in the employ of the British Museum of Natural History, asking for an opinion. Mr Thomas in turn forwarded Major Cooper's letter and photograph to Mr R.I. Pocock, Curator of Mammals at the British Museum, and this photograph, together with Major Cooper's account of the skin he had examined, was published in *The Field* of 14th October 1926. Mr Pocock, after examining the small photograph, put forward the theory that it was an aberrant leopard, and published his reply to Major Cooper, together with reproductions of other aberrant specimens, in an article in *The Field* of 21st October, 1926.

Major Cooper, in the meantime, had been making extensive enquiries, and finally got in touch with Mr H.M.G. Jackson, Assistant Chief Native Commissioner, who informed Major Cooper that he had seen a similar skin at the Mutambara Mission, near Melsetter. A native police sergeant in the employ of Mr Jackson, when shown the skin, said that he knew the animal and described its habits, mentioning its extreme shyness and the fact that it would not attack domestic animals, except perhaps a young kid. It was also established that the natives were not at all afraid of this animal, as they were of a leopard, and would attack it armed only with assegais. This indicates that the animal was more like a cheetah in behaviour than a leopard. Major Cooper, greatly interested in this matter, thereafter approached Sir Herbert Taylor, then Chief Native Commissioner, for assistance, and in due course all Native Commissioners were requested to report any available further information about this animal. From these further investigations it was revealed that Mr Watters, a former Native Commissioner at Bikita, possessed two king cheetah skins, presumably obtained in his district. These skins were photographed, and Miss Daphne Hills of the Zoological Department at the British Museum of Natural History, informs me that this photograph, together with two other identical photographs, is in the possession of the Museum. A Mr Lacey of Salisbury also possessed such a skin, which he had obtained from natives in the Seki (or Siki) Reserve, which is situated about 30 km south of Salisbury. All these skins proved to be similarly patterned, not spotted, but having "curiously raised or embossed stripes", wrote Major Cooper. All five skins found by Cooper were procured in different places at different times "which pretty well disposes of the theory of the skin being that of an aberrant animal" he remarked at the time.

Cooper was far from satisfied with Mr Pocock's opinion that the new discovery was an aberrant leopard, and communicated with him again, placing before him the further evidence which he had collected. Major Cooper

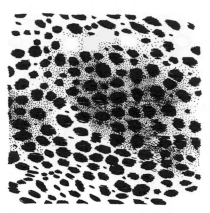
Common Cheetah

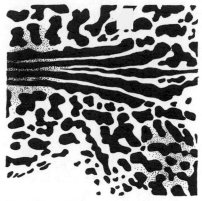
King Cheetah

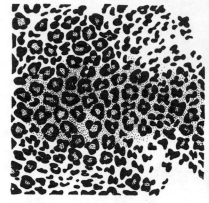
Leopard

Diagram showing markings of pelage

requested, and was given, permission by the Committee of the Queen Victoria Memorial Library and Museum to send the skin in their possession to Mr Pocock for examination. Cooper strongly suggested to Pocock that this was a new species of Felidae, and with the further facts before him, and after an examination of the skin sent from the Museum in Salisbury, it became clear to Pocock that his initial theory of an aberrant leopard must fall away. His reasons for assigning the animal to the genus *Acinonyx* were based on a number of differences between the cheetah and the leopard. Briefly, they are the structure of the feet, which are completely identical to those of the common cheetah and differ entirely from the leopard; the presence of the mane on the nape of the neck (which was indistinguishable in the small photograph he had previously examined), which is absent in the leopard; the unspotted belly of the common cheetah, whereas in leopard the belly is fully spotted; and the characteristic tear line present in cheetah. Pocock could find no evidence from the skin he examined that the king cheetah was more heavily built than the common cheetah, as previously mentioned by Cooper, since the measurements of the two species appeared to correspond closely.

So it was that in 1927 this animal was named *Acinonyx rex* by Pocock, being accorded the status of a new species.

It has always been accepted in scientific literature that the type locality (the area from which the first discovery originates) of *A. rex* is Umvukwe, an area situated to the north of Salisbury. However, this is incorrect, the type locality being in fact Macheke, a town to the southeast of Salisbury. How the localities came to be confused is not apparent, but information kindly provided by Dr Smithers makes the situation clear. To re-cap in brief: in his account of the king cheetah, Major Cooper clearly states that he sent a photograph of the skin in the possession of the Museum in Salisbury to Mr Pocock. Sir Clarkson Tredgold had shown Cooper the skin telling him that this skin was presented to the Museum by Mr Donald Fraser. Fraser, who resided at a place called Headlands, had purchased it from natives who had shot the animal in the Macheke District, which is about 32 km to the north of Headlands. It was this

18

skin which Cooper, with permission from the Museum, sent to Pocock for examination. Dr Smithers, presently director of the National Museums and Monuments of Rhodesia, informs me that the granting of this permission is recorded in the Minutes of the Annual Meeting of subscribers to the Queen Victoria Memorial Library and Museum, dated 13th July 1927, in which ". . . The Chairman spoke of a new species of cheetah discovered through the interest of Major Cooper, a member of the committee". A newspaper report which covered this Annual Meeting states ". . . a cheetah skin presented by Mr Donald Fraser of Headlands proved to be a new species. Major A.L. Cooper with permission of the committee had the skin sent to the Natural History Museum for identification. It has been named *Acinonyx rex* to emphasise the splendour of its livery . . .".

Further evidence which indicates that the type locality of *A. rex* is Macheke comes from Dr Smithers himself who, for many years, has been deeply interested in the history of king cheetah. In about 1947 he photographed the Macheke skin, which was displayed on a wall in the Queen Victoria Museum. This photograph and the photograph of the skin in Pocock's paper of 1927, in which Pocock said that the skin came from Umvukwe, are identical. Moreover, the article on the king cheetah written by Major Cooper in 1927 includes a photograph of the Macheke skin sent to Pocock; this photograph is identical to the photograph in Pocock's paper, and identical to the Macheke skin which Dr Smithers himself photographed. There can be no doubt that Pocock was incorrect, due possibly to some misunderstanding, and the type locality of *A. rex* should have read Macheke, not Umvukwe. Unfortunately, the Macheke skin, designated the *holotype,* cannot now be traced, either having been destroyed or lost, which as Dr Smithers says is a zoological tragedy because a type skin is an extremely valuable specimen. The skull of this holotype does not exist.

Previously (up to the 1940's), it was thought that king cheetah occurred only in Rhodesia, and it seems strange that this animal was never mentioned by the observant early hunters such as Selous and van Niekerk, since its distribution, up to that time, covered a fairly large and inhabited part of Rhodesia. Then in 1958, the editor of a newspaper in the Transvaal, South Africa, commented on the matter of the king cheetah, and as a result, readers reported having seen the king cheetah in the northern sector of the Kruger National Park, and in parts of the northern Transvaal. A skin was subsequently located on the farm "Kongo", near Messina, in the possession of Mr S. van der Walt, who had shot the animal in 1940. The markings on the skin were consistent with the markings of a specimen of a king cheetah taken in Rhodesia. But early in 1973, Dr U. de V. Pienaar, informed me that the king cheetah had never been recorded as occurring in the Kruger National Park, and that the sighting of a "king cheetah" at the old Olifants camp (Balule) turned out to be a civet cat.

There are records of king cheetah occurring in Botswana and Dr Smithers, who conducted a mammal survey there, found a king cheetah skin in the possession of a storekeeper at Moyabana, west of Serowe. This skin now forms part of the collection of the National Museum at Gaborone in Botswana.

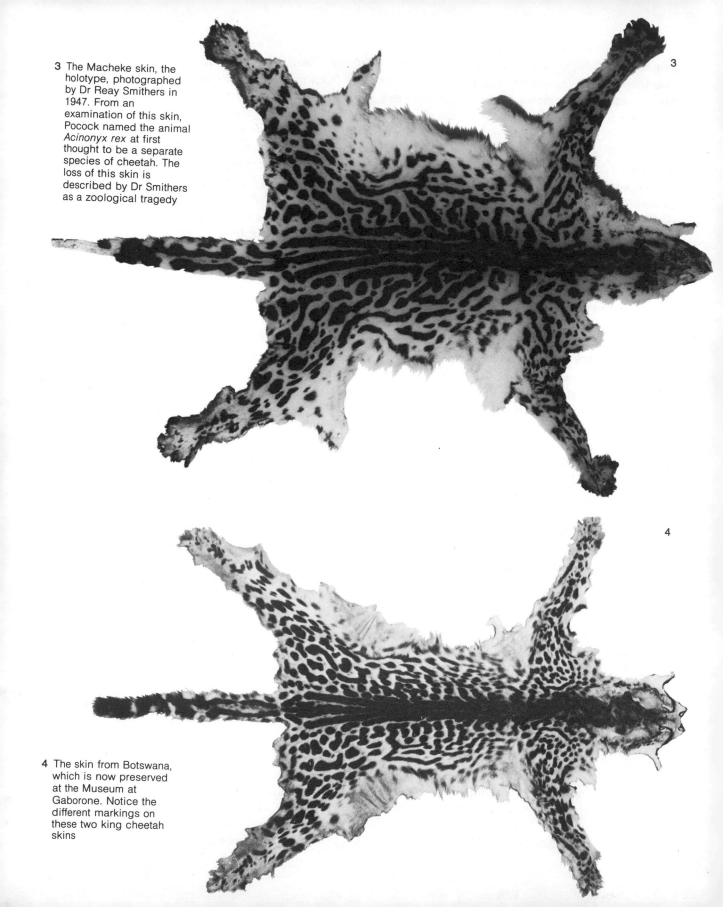

3 The Macheke skin, the holotype, photographed by Dr Reay Smithers in 1947. From an examination of this skin, Pocock named the animal *Acinonyx rex* at first thought to be a separate species of cheetah. The loss of this skin is described by Dr Smithers as a zoological tragedy

4 The skin from Botswana, which is now preserved at the Museum at Gaborone. Notice the different markings on these two king cheetah skins

Another king cheetah skin was found by Dr Smithers in a store at Lobatsi, and was later sold in Johannesburg. Two king cheetah were sighted on van Riet's farm in the southern Tuli Block by a Mr Challis, whom Dr Smithers describes as a reliable observer.

Having considered all these various sightings and the origins of the different skins, I began to wonder about their present whereabouts. Were they still in existence, and where did those skins which had been mounted come from? I wrote to a number of people on this matter, and as a result, some new and interesting facts have recently emerged regarding the two skins in the Bikita photograph, which for many years were thought to be missing. This photograph was also sent to Mr Pocock by Major Cooper. Daphne Hills, in a letter to me, describes the photograph as showing a man holding up two flat skins, and until recently, the whereabouts of these skins was unknown. Dr J. Pringle, when approached about the origin of the mounted specimen at Natal Museum in Pietermaritzburg, told me that it was purchased from Rowland Ward, Taxidermists in London, who informed the Natal Museum that it came from the "Macheke District and Seki Reserve". The British Museum (Natural History) possesses a mounted specimen, the tag on which reads only "S. Rhodesia". As a result of my enquiry, Hills undertook extensive research regarding king cheetah skins and her detailed examination of the photograph of the two Bikita skins revealed that they are indeed not missing. As I mentioned earlier, each "king" skin has its own individual pattern, and by comparing the markings of the two Bikita skins in the photograph with those of the two mounted specimens (whose localities were vague) Hills established that the mounted specimen at Natal Museum is one of the Bikita skins and the mounted specimen at the British Museum is the other. Further, it had always been thought that only two skins originated from the Bikita district. But a photograph of a mounted specimen taken by Rowland Ward proves the existence of a third skin, also collected by Mr Watters in the Bikita district. This is the mounted specimen in the South African Museum in Cape Town.

Obviously, inadequate early records of origination and a very loose use of place names created the confusion regarding the historical localities of king cheetah skins. Roberts, in his book on the mammals of South Africa, mentions five skins originating from Melsetter, but unfortunately he gives no further details. As only one skin has actually been recorded from Melsetter, it is possible that Roberts lumped together records of skins taken near and around Melsetter (see map). Shortridge notes that "striped cheetah" were recorded from Ndanga and Nuanetse, but no further details are mentioned and I have not been able to obtain confirmation of any king cheetah being taken in these areas.

To date then, twelve specimens and six sightings have been recorded, and the photograph taken of a king cheetah in 1974 in the Kruger National Park means that this mutation has occurred over at least five decades. An interesting fact emerges from the records of some of the sightings. In one instance, four cheetah were seen together in a group, but only one was a *king*. Another sighting recorded by a Mr Buckmaster in 1928 was of a male and a female king

Locality records of King Cheetah

X specimens taken
O sightings

cheetah; I wonder if these two *kings* were from the same litter? The sighting of the two *kings* on a farm in the southern Tuli Block in Botswana by Mr Challis again raises this query. And if these animals were fairly numerous early in this century why is no mention made of them by the early hunters and inhabitants? Hunters more especially had a keen eye for anything unusual or different and if king cheetah were common they would surely have come across them and recorded such facts, for most of the early hunters kept meticulous records of their various encounters. One would assume that the unusual markings of a king

22

Table I: *Historical localities of specimens taken of king cheetah*

DATE[1]	LOCALITY	SPECIMEN	COLLECTOR[2]	PRESENT OWNER
1926	Macheke district, Rhodesia	Flat skin (the holotype)	Mr D. Fraser	National Museums & Monuments of Rhodesia[3]
1925	Bikita, Rhodesia	Mounted skin	Mr H. N. Watters	British Museum (Natural History), London
1925	Bikita, Rhodesia	Mounted skin	Mr H. N. Watters	Natal Museum, P.M.Burg, S.A.
1925?	Melsetter, Mutambara Mission, Rhodesia	Flat skin	Unknown	Unknown
1926	Seki Reserve, Rhodesia	Flat skin	Mr Lacey	Unknown
1927	Mt Selinda, Rhodesia	Mounted skin	Major A. L. Cooper	British Museum (Natural History), London
1928	Bikita, Rhodesia	Mounted skin	Mr H. N. Watters	S.A. Museum, Cape Town, S.A.
1935	Sabi, Rhodesia	Flat skin	Mr D. Townley	Privately owned
1940	Messina, South Africa	Flat skin	Mr S. van der Walt	Unknown
1950?	Botswana, exact locality unknown	Flat skin	Mr Stan Lester	Skin made up into a jacket, photograph in existence
1970?	Botswana, exact locality unknown	Flat skin?	Unknown	Unknown (sold in Johannesburg in about 1970)
1971	Moyabana, Botswana	Flat skin	Dr R. H. N. Smithers	National Museum of Botswana

1: This is the collection date and not necessarily the date when the specimen was taken
2: In most cases the Collector obtained the skin from local tribesmen
3: See page 19

cheetah would immediately draw the observer's attention to it, yet the late Stan Lester of Lobatsi in Botswana, who knew his wildlife, did not know he had shot a king cheetah until he examined the carcass.

Dr Smithers feels sure that king cheetah will continue to turn up during the course of time wherever there are cheetah, but he does stress that sightings must be carefully evaluated, as in many instances the serval, which has a certain similarity in its markings, has been mistaken for a king cheetah. In this vein, Major Cooper received a letter after the publication of Pocock's article in *The*

Field indicating that the writer had handled many king cheetah skins which, he said, were of "African ocelot". The ocelot is not indigenous to the continent of Africa so it may be that the writer of the letter confused ocelot with serval.

When king cheetah were first discovered, it was thought at that time that a skull of this animal, when found, may show some differences between *jubatus* and *rex*. Roberts records the existence of two king cheetah skulls and gives their measurements. The one skull, acquired by the Vernay-Lang Kalahari Expedition in 1930 is in the possession of the Field Museum in Chicago and Hills has established that this skull is in fact that of a common cheetah. Dr Smithers informs me that the other skull is still in existence but the records at the Queen Victoria Memorial Library and Museum do not indicate its provenance, "and it might well be an ordinary cheetah". But Dr Smithers adds that even if there were available a number of king cheetah skulls he doubts if any difference would be found between the structure and characteristics of the skulls of *jubatus* and *rex* "anymore than there is between an ordinary leopard and the very many aberrant leopards that one comes across". The present taxonomic nomenclature does not recognise the king cheetah as a distinct species, or even as a sub-species, but classifies this animal as an aberrant form of the common cheetah.

But the name stays. This spectacular mutation can hardly be described as anything but a *king* cheetah.

4 The Cursorial Felid

Some years ago I saw a film called *The African Elephant,* in which there was a sequence of a cheetah taking a prey animal. A little crouching, a little stalking, then suddenly the cheetah took off. The speed with which this animal moved was very apparent in this sequence; at a tremendous rate it countered the dodging of the gazelle, accelerating and making turns as if it were born to this particular activity, as indeed it is. I wondered . . . how does it attain such a speed? What enables it to accelerate so quickly, to turn so sharply, to stop so suddenly? For me, learning of the many physical adaptations of this remarkable animal proved fascinating in the extreme. Every conceivable part of the cheetah is designed for running. It is a creature built and equipped for acceleration and speed; the speed of a fast running cheetah has been recorded at 110–114 km an hour. It can accelerate rapidly, and claims have been made that a cheetah can reach a speed of 72 km an hour from a standing position in a matter of two seconds.

People are often sceptical about the reports and maintain that it is impossible for any living creature to reach such speeds. However, running cheetah have been timed, and there is a record of a cheetah covering more than 630 metres in 20 seconds, which is slightly more than 114 km an hour. And in the United States in 1969, Kurt Severin trained a cheetah to pursue bait that was pulled along the ground at high speeds. The distance the cheetah was to run was demarcated and the time it took the cheetah to cover this distance was recorded by means of stop watches. This was done several times, and the top speed was 114 km an hour. Without doubt, the validity of these performances is unassailable. Many people are convinced that the swiftness of cheetah is exaggerated, and that those few that have been timed to exceed 110 km an hour are the exception rather than the rule. In London a cheetah was timed over 450 metres on an oval track and it only reached 71 km an hour, and on a straight 400 metre run the speed was 72 km an hour. After tests with cheetah chasing an electric hare on a dog race track, a "general speed" of 71 km an hour was noted. Motorists have mentioned cheetah running at up to 96 km an hour, and one animal remained ahead of a car travelling at 80 km an hour for about 180 metres, but this cheetah gave the impression of not trying very hard. In the Serengeti, speeds of 88 km an hour were recorded but the observers felt that the cheetah could attain higher speeds during short bursts, as is evidenced by another record of a cheetah doing a dash at between 104 and 112 km an hour.

During the twenties and thirties some attempts were made to race cheetah and greyhounds on a race track in England, at Harringay near London. Although the cheetah were faster than the greyhounds, recorded speeds were only in the region of 70 km an hour. I was amused to learn that this racing ended in failure because while the greyhounds methodically pursued the hare around the oval

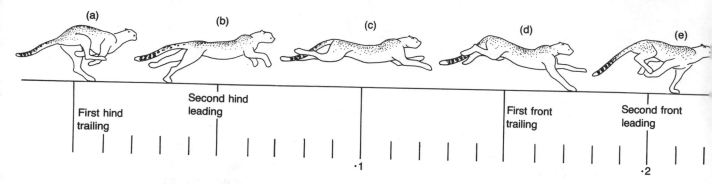

(a)   (b)   (c)   (d)   (e)

First hind trailing

Second hind leading

First front trailing

Second front leading

·1   ·2

Body positions in the stride of a running cheetah (after Hildebrand 1960) Time: Seconds (running at 90 km/h)

track, the cheetah soon realised that a short cut across the oval was far more intelligent.

Obviously though, the speeds of individual cheetah will vary. But I would think that the difference in the conditions under which cheetah have been observed and timed would be the factor exerting the greatest influence over the results of speed tests. Cheetah run for various reasons, and since they have been timed at around 114 km an hour there are obviously instances when they will run an awful lot faster than they seem to do around a track. They probably have a very good understanding of the difference between an electric hare and a real live gazelle. Professor Grzimek writes of the swiftness of one of the cheetah at Frankfurt Zoo in Germany; this animal could catch wild rabbits from a distance of 36 metres before the rabbits could cover the four or five metres to their burrows. "Its initial velocity is astounding – it shoots forward like an arrow from a bow."

Before we examine how a cheetah achieves its speed, we need to consider a few basics. To be really fast, a runner must take long and rapid strides. Although some animals have long legs it does not necessarily follow that they can travel at a high speed. The giraffe is a good example. It has long legs and can achieve a long stride, but its rate of stride is slow, resulting in only a moderate speed. Conversely the warthog, with much shorter legs than a giraffe, runs at about the same speed, taking shorter strides but at a much more rapid rate. A cheetah, with its long slender limbs and specialised adaptations, achieves both a long and a rapid stride, and this combination enables the cheetah to travel so swiftly. At this point it may be as well to explain what is meant by the word *stride.* In one stride a running cheetah completes usually seven phases, or motions. This is made up of five supported phases, in which one or more limbs are in contact with the ground, and two unsupported phases, the limbs in these instances are off the ground. Dr Milton Hildebrand, who has made a study of cheetah locomotion, believes that there is sometimes a third, fleeting period of suspension (an eighth phase) in one stride. This period occurs in a position between (d) and (e) in the sequence of drawings at the top of this page. It must be emphasised, however, that not every cheetah will necessarily follow the precise pattern of the diagrams at all times because there are various factors which will influence each running cheetah, such as terrain or the type of prey species it is chasing.

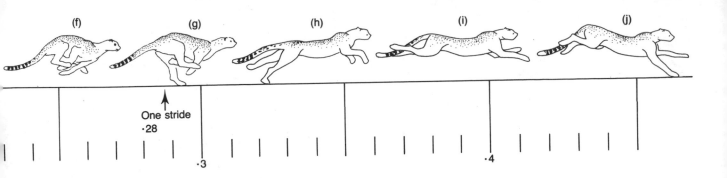

One stride
·28

·3

·4

In a fast gallop the rotary, or lateral movement is employed by cheetah. This is, in effect, a sequence of footfalls in which each of the leading and trailing forefeet are followed by the hindfeet on the same side of the animal's body. The leading foot is not the limb that strikes the ground first, but rather it is the limb that reaches out the furthest and is the second of the fore or hind feet to strike and leave the ground in a phase. When a cheetah is in a fully flexed position, see (f), both hindlegs are swung far forward of the body and the forelegs are pushed backwards. In this position the animal must avoid interference between hind and forelegs, and the cheetah overcomes this problem by straddling the forelegs with the hindlegs. For comparison, consider a horse which uses a transverse gallop. Since the legs of a horse have little lateral motion, the hindlegs cannot straddle the forelegs, thus each foreleg is followed by the hindleg on the opposite side of its body. Although one would think that the rotary sequence of footfalls would increase the reach of the limbs, Hildebrand considers this not to be the case. He feels that the exact benefit derived from the use of the rotary gallop is not altogether clear and he comments, "perhaps the rotary sequence provides subtle benefits to balance or muscle function". I think it reasonable to surmise that the rotary gallop provides for greater flexion of the spine than would otherwise be possible, since the straddling of the forelegs allows both hindlegs to reach their extreme forward position simultaneously.

Two periods of suspension in the stride of a running cheetah (after Hildebrand 1960)

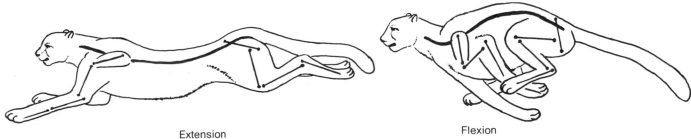

Extension

Flexion

Note the rotation of the scapula on the spine

27

When the trailing foreleg strikes the ground, the forequarters and hindquarters are moving at the same speed. When the front feet are on the ground, the body is flexed on the forelimbs, and at the instant that the leading foot leaves the ground, the hindquarters have greater forward velocity than the forequarters, to attain maximum flexion during the following period of suspension, position (f). Hildebrand makes an interesting calculation regarding the extended phase of a stride. A running cheetah only extends its back after the hind feet strike the ground, and "executes this manoeuvre so adeptly that it could run at about six miles (ten km) an hour without any legs". The extremely supple spine, through its flexion and extension, makes a double contribution to the cheetah's speed. The length of a stride is increased by up to 76 cm at high speeds, adding approximately an extra ten km an hour, and the rate of stride is also increased through the attainment of a greater forward velocity in the swing of the limbs. Generally, movement and swing of fore- and hindlimbs is accomplished almost exclusively by a single group of muscles attached to these limbs, but a significant difference in cheetah is that the muscles of the back also contribute towards this movement. The cheetah then has two independent sets of muscles which act simultaneously, and so provide a greater force than would one group of muscles. Certain muscles attached to the scapula are, in a cheetah, horizontally oriented whereas for example, in a leopard, these muscles are vertically oriented. The cheetah derives the benefit of a powerful oscillation of the scapula which contributes to the rapidity of its rate of stride; the leopard requires strength for vertical climbing movements, especially needed for hauling a heavy meal up a tree.

To add further to the ease with which a cheetah attains a long stride, the scapula, which is more elongated than in other felids, has unusually great freedom of movement, being able to pivot on the spine through about 26° with the swing of the leg and the extreme length of stride means that the forelegs will strike the ground at an acute angle, (i) and (j). To prevent an excessive up and down movement as the shoulders pass over the feet, the leg joints are flexed, the scapula rising in relation to the cheetah's back.

The rotation of the hips and shoulders, the extreme suppleness of the spine, and the greater swing of the legs which strike and leave the ground at

Table II: *Speed, lengths and durations of stride of running cheetah*

	CHEETAH 1	CHEETAH 2	% CHANGE
Average speed	53 km/hr	90 km/hr	70
Average length of stride	4,35 metres	7 metres	61
Average duration of stride	0,31 sec.	0,28 sec.	10

Dr R. F. Ewer, using the results of Hildebrand's calculations, mentions that to achieve 112 km an hour the length of stride would be in the region of 9,14 metres

5 & 6 Extreme freedom of
movement of the
scapula causes the
hump at the
shoulders

7

8

7 & 8 Threat to man.
Note the raised
tail and
splayed toes
9 & 10 There is no
record of a
cheetah
making a
deliberate
attack on
man

9   10

acute angles all contribute towards a long and rapid stride. The duration of the phases of a stride will vary between individual cheetah, but generally, as a cheetah accelerates from a slow to a fast run, the length of stride increases substantially while the rate of stride increases only slightly. Having analysed a film strip of a running cheetah in the Walt Disney film *African Lion,* and compared this to the analysis of a film taken by himself at Ocala, Florida, Hildebrand calculated running speed, lengths and durations of stride for each of the two cheetah. These results I have tabulated, and calculated the percentage by which each factor changed from the Walt Disney cheetah (cheetah 1) running relatively slowly, to the Ocala cheetah (cheetah 2) running fast.

Uneven terrain, prevention of fatigue occasioned by the use of the same leading forefoot, and a dodging quarry are factors which determine that a running cheetah must change lead while in motion. (When running, an animal can turn more sharply if it leads with its inside forefoot.) A cheetah can initiate a change in lead in the split second following the period of suspension as shown in position (c), since this position immediately precedes the placement of the trailing forefoot (the first one to strike the ground) and thus the cheetah need not anticipate too far in advance a change of lead which may be necessitated by the sudden turn of a dodging prey animal. Changes in lead are so smoothly accomplished that the cheetah suffers little (if any at all) loss of speed during this subtle manoeuvre. A running cheetah is not easily thrown off balance by its dodging prey, but timing the change of lead is of the utmost importance, and it does happen that a cheetah running at full speed fails to anticipate a sudden, sharp dodge. The result of course can be a lost meal. Hildebrand initially surmised that the frequent changes in lead were possibly due to irregular or uneven terrain or a sudden change in the direction of travel. From a subsequent study, undertaken at Ocala, Florida, where a captive cheetah was able to run in a 60 metre long enclosure, he found that this cheetah changed lead frequently, even when running on a straight and "unobstructed" track.

From a speed of over 32 km an hour a cheetah is able to stop in one single stride. The two front feet strike the ground more or less simultaneously, thereafter the hindfeet strike the ground and "all four feet are placed far to the front and the toes are spread". The captive cheetah at Ocala ended its 60 metre long chase by turning sharply around a tree which was situated at the end of the track. From an average of four observations Hildebrand concluded: "On these runs the animal's body leans into the turn to such an extent that its dorso-ventral axis forms an angle of only about 29° with the ground". The tail was often raised just prior to these sharp turns, but Hildebrand could find no evidence that the tail aided the movement of the body in turning. This is surprising because other opinions have been expressed to the effect that a cheetah's tail, which is approximately half the length of its body, does in fact act as a balancer or rudder which assists this animal to make sharp turns.

Cheetah have digitigrade feet, which means they walk on their toes, not on the whole foot, and the bone structure is adapted to withstand the force of a hard run and to enable the animal to perform sharp and sudden turns. The pads

31

of the toes (the digital and metacarpal pads) are also modified, being hard and pointed which is perhaps an adaptation to the need for sudden braking, and the palmar pads have longitudinal ridges, acting in the manner of tyre treads.

While walking and trotting cheetah use the rotary movement as for the gallop, but the length of stride is much shorter. A walking cheetah completes eight phases in one stride, covering a distance of about 1,35 metres per stride, and moving at about 4,7 km an hour. The body of a walking cheetah is supported by two, three or all four feet, so that, proportionately per stride, the feet are on the ground for a longer time than when running. In the trot, which is "erect, symmetrical and springy" slightly longer strides are taken than in the walk; 1,93 metres per stride, again with eight phases completed. A cheetah can travel at about 21 km an hour while trotting and the body is supported by one or two limbs at a time, and it may have an unsupported phase as well. Minimal effort is utilised by a cheetah when walking. Here, efficiency is the main consideration whereas in running, speed is the main consideration. When walking a cheetah conserves its energy and in its short bursts at high speed expends its energy fully. "The cheetah does not need to be efficient, it needs to be fast," says Hildebrand.

The cheetah's body posture varies quite considerably at different speeds. The cheetah at Ocala had been trained to chase bait, in the form of meat, in a 60 metre long enclosure. Although in some of the experiments the animal could easily have taken the bait before the end of the track, at times it ran beside the bait and only took the meat at the end of the run. At other times the cheetah approached the bait closely, and then ran forward in a low crouch, and on other occasions it ran "with shoulders and pelvis bobbing up and down in the extreme". This cheetah ran easily while looking back over one of its shoulders, and Hildebrand recorded that, on occasion, it "ran slowly sideways by alternately bouncing the fore- and hindquarters to one side".

So a cheetah runs. "The observer is impressed by the animal's agility, flexibility, co-ordination, and lithe flowing motions," writes Hildebrand. Taken together, these adaptations make the cheetah unique. It is programmed for speed. There is no replacement for the cheetah. We can't afford to lose it.

A cheetah bares its teeth

A cheetah threatens the photographer

5 Hunting

It is early morning. The sun hardly shows over the horizon, but already the creatures of daylight are astir, and a predator is out in search of food. A female cheetah has perched herself on a mound of earth. She sits patiently, alert. Nearby a small herd of impala are browsing. The cheetah quietly drops from her elevated perch and walks slowly towards the herd. There is ample cover in the form of bushes and shrubs and she makes full use of this to approach unseen to within striking distance of her prey. Stalking silently with body lowered the cheetah advances. At about 50 metres she rises up and without further ado streaks forward. At this same moment another cheetah in a distant and different habitat has spotted a hare, and leaving out all preliminaries dashes after it. With acute agility the hunter negotiates a tight figure-of-eight turn in the wake of the hare, and seizes it. In a third area, a similar scene is being enacted on this same morning. A cheetah has discovered a herd of Thomson's gazelle and slowly moves forward, her head slightly lowered. The herd shows signs of restlessness. The cheetah sits down in the grass and waits. Seconds pass and again the cheetah moves forward. There is almost no cover and the predator is now about 100 metres from the herd. She is even more cautious now, pausing whenever the gazelles show their uneasiness. The moment is tense as the predator quickens her pace then suddenly shoots forward straight for a gazelle that has strayed a little way from the others.

The Kruger National Park, the Kalahari Gemsbok National Park and the Serengeti; three vastly different environments, each containing its own varying complement of prey species. And in each the cheetah hunts with precision, from the sand dunes of the Kalahari to the parkland savannah of the Kruger National Park, to the open grassland in the Serengeti. Cheetah hunt in a variety of habitats and employ a wide range of methods to capture their prey. In grassland, woodland, arid and semi-arid biomes, cheetah hunt prey ranging from Thomson's gazelle to hare, from did-dik to steenbok, from guinea fowl to ostrich. A cheetah may stalk its prey, it may casually walk towards its prey, or it may simply dash straight at its prey, but it is the habitat and the prey species which largely determine the method to be used.

Felids evince three basic characteristics in their hunting and killing methods. They are, in brief, stalking (if cover is available), the use of a forepaw to overthrow prey, and the throat or neck bite. Cheetah, descendants of the Miacidae which roamed our continents some 60 million years ago, have over the ages modified the three basic hunting and killing techniques used by their early ancestors. Adapting to changing circumstances, they have also evolved specialised physical adaptations suitable to their particular hunting methods. The throat bite (rather than the neck bite) now employed by cheetah is one such modification, and the skilful use of the forepaw, aided by the dew claw, is another. At times, both forepaws may be used to bring down prey. The modifications and physical adaptations indicate that within the Felidae, cheetah have diverged from the other felids in their hunting and killing techniques. Physical characteristics, such as the various adaptations for speed are further evidence that this animal "is no evolutionary upstart but has been at the game for a considerable time" writes Dr R.F. Ewer in her recent and comprehensive work *The Carnivores*.

Extremely keen eyesight is a benefit which the cheetah enjoys, and these animals appear to take little or no cognisance of the wind when hunting. Because cheetah hunt predominantly by sight, most of their hunting activities are confined to the daytime, (early morning and late afternoon being the preferred period), though sometimes, if there is bright moonlight, the cheetah may also hunt at night. A cheetah spends most of the day resting under shady trees, and sometimes perches on top of a mound of earth, or takes up some other elevated position, possibly searching for herds of prey animals. Cheetah are not known as tree climbers in the sense that one thinks of leopard shinning up and down trees, although they may take advantage of low branches in order to gain elevation. Cheetah do jump up on to low branches to urinate or defecate, but when up in a tree, a cheetah does look clumsy. I once saw a cheetah leap effortlessly into a tree and then spend a good few minutes trying to get into a dignified position, but without success, whereupon it jumped down and ambled off. It made me think of a rather endearing story Willie Labuschagne told me about a cheetah who decided to take a nap in a tree, balancing its body rather precariously on a branch. In a very short while the sleeping cheetah came down to earth with a thump and although Willie was amused the cheetah, I should imagine, was not. Cheetah do not travel any great distance in search of a meal, but rather wait for prey herds to come close to them. In the Serengeti they generally travel about three to five km a day, but in this area prey herds are plentiful so there is no need for extensive foraging. If prey herds are scattered over a great area, the cheetah must, of necessity, move in search of them, and of course, since cheetah tend to follow migratory prey herds, there are times when they will travel extensively. A female cheetah with newly born cubs is, to a certain extent, restricted in her movements, until such time as the cubs are able to follow her when she is hunting. The first few weeks for a female with cubs must be a bit rough. She must eat, her ability to suckle her young depends on her physical condition, but if prey herds are scattered this can mean leaving the defenceless young for fairly long periods, and very often the cubs provide a meal for passing predators.

Cheetah hunting Thomson's gazelle in the Serengeti commonly stalk their victims and this stalking with the cheetah in a crouched position, body and head held low, may last for anything up to half an hour. This is not to say that no other methods are used. Sometimes a cheetah merely walks toward a herd of these gazelle without any attempt at concealment. The gazelle watch the cheetah carefully and usually take flight when it has come to within 100–300 metres. Then after fleeing only a short distance, if not pursued, they stop and even retrace their steps a little way. This "behaviour of fascination" has been observed predominantly in relation to cheetah and leopard. The gazelle recognise a predator at distances of up to 800 metres and they may then approach to within one or two hundred metres of the predator. They tend to maintain this distance and even follow the predator if it moves. Predators other than cheetah (except the wild dog) are allowed to approach to within a much lesser distance before the gazelle take flight. A cheetah tends to select as its quarry that individual which takes to flight first and that individual is very often an adult female or a subadult of either sex.

Professor Fritz Walther, who studied Thomson's gazelle in the Serengeti for two years, has described hunts in which cheetah approach a gazelle herd, coming as close as possible, using cover if this is available. When the Thomson's gazelle detect the predator they immediately become alert, at which point the cheetah stops and stands motionless, or even sits down. Then it suddenly breaks into a very fast run, and on overtaking the herd, pursues one animal. During the chase, other gazelle may cross the cheetah's path and sometimes it may run beside other gazelle, and even pass through an entire herd, but it continues to pursue the pre-selected animal, the one that took to flight first. The apparent selection of females and subadults must of course depend on the composition of a gazelle herd, which can vary from day to day. Obviously, the contention is not that cheetah actively select females, but rather that they tend to pursue an animal that takes to flight first, and if, in a bachelor herd, one adult male flees first, the cheetah will probably pursue that animal. It seems that cheetah find it difficult not to pursue an animal that runs away from it as this probably acts as a stimulus which releases the predatory sequence.

In some cases stalking plays a minor role in a cheetah hunt, and a very fast chase, culminating in the victim being overturned by the cheetah's forepaw constitutes the major element of the hunting method. If a cheetah is to stalk its intended quarry then the habitat must lend itself to this behaviour, providing cover in the form of tall grass, small bushes or even branches that have fallen from trees. But the vegetation may not always provide adequate cover for stalking, as in the case of some parts of the Kalahari Gemsbok National Park. Rolling sand dunes stretch out before one's eyes, almost never ending, and the vegetation for the most part is quite sparse, until one reaches the Nossob and Auob Rivers, which are more densely wooded areas. Cheetah in the Kalahari, says Labuschagne, do not always employ specific hunting techniques, and in most instances they simply launch an attack. But when cheetah approach a prey herd, while not stalking in "classic" fashion, if ground cover is available this is used to the best advantage.

Watching a cheetah stalk can be fascinating, especially if one is on the receiving end, as I discovered on my first visit to De Wildt Estates, an experimental cheetah breeding farm to the north of Pretoria. Our two vehicles were driven into the 40 hectare cheetah enclosure, and after the cheetah had been fed, we stood, still in the enclosure, talking about these remarkable animals. Godfrey van Dyk (who owns the farm) and I were some little distance from the vehicles when I glanced up, straight into the eyes of a large and somewhat temperamental male cheetah. The cheetah was about 20 metres from me, and with his eyes rivetted on my face, he slowly moved towards me. Standing absolutely still, I stared at this animal, completely fascinated. His large amber eyes didn't flicker once, his face was quite without expression, and it was an effort for me to take my eyes off him, as I felt all but mesmerized. A human semi-circle was quickly formed between this cheetah and myself (but I had a

strong feeling that he just looked straight through it) and I was manoeuvred back to the vehicles. This was a determined creature, however, and he proceeded to move towards where I was now standing, and even tried a detour to approach me from behind the semi-circle. It was only when we were preparing to leave the enclosure and climbed into the vehicles that this cheetah lost interest.

To what extent stalking is innate is debatable. Cubs at play often stalk their "victims", approaching from behind some sort of cover with bodies lowered to the ground. Kruuk and Turner conclude that "As in many carnivores, this play behaviour could reflect hunting methods". But Eaton has said that in the open shortgrass plains in the Serengeti, cheetah cubs will stalk, but adult cheetah seldom do, which could indicate that stalking "as a portion of the innate predatory sequence, must drop out with hunting experience". One must remember though, that the local habitat is one of the determining factors of the cheetah's hunting method. Where little if any cover is available, stalking becomes relatively less important.

Sir Archibald James, former big game hunter and one of the original members of the British and Rhodesian Fauna Preservation Societies, wrote me of an incident which took place in Rhodesia some years back. A hunting party found three young cheetah cubs, one of which was sickly and subsequently died. One of the others, a female, was raised by the son of a veterinary surgeon and became devoted to his two large alsatians. The cub romped about with them, but one day it began to play at killing them. It did this by running alongside the dog and adeptly putting a foreleg between the dog's paws, causing the dog to somersault. The cheetah then seized the dog by the throat, but carried the predatory sequence no further, as it would do in a real hunt. This cub was not raised by its mother and was therefore not "taught" how to hunt, but that it

37

employed hunting tactics used by wild cheetah, is of interest, for the question one then asks is, "How much is learned, and how much is innate?" Pertinent to this is the coursing of cheetah by the Moghuls of India. Only adult cheetah from the wild were used to hunt black buck, as it was believed that in the process of reaching adulthood cheetah learned the art of hunting from their mothers.

So much for stalking, and we now turn our attention to other methods of hunting employed by cheetah. Parts of the Nairobi National Park in Kenya comprise open shortgrass plains, which by their very nature lend themselves to an open pursuit method, rather than elaborate stalking. Sometimes, cheetah simply dash at a herd from a distance of about 100 to 200 metres. Its great speed brings the predator close enough to select a prey animal from the herd which it then pursues with undivided attention. On the open plains of this Park, the main diet of two particular cheetah was the kongoni (red hartebeest) and the method of hunting employed by them was simply to walk toward the prey herd. When they had closed to about 50 metres, a yearling kongoni invariably turned to face the oncoming predators and proceeded to "attack" them, in so doing coming about 20 metres closer to the two predators, who then launched their swift and final attack. This specialisation by these two cheetah may well have been the result of a learned behaviour, says Eaton, the anti-predator attack making the kongoni vulnerable.

It is perfectly conceivable that a cheetah will adapt and modify its techniques when hunting different prey species. This is illustrated by the example of the kongoni. Another fine example is cheetah hunting ostrich. I well remember my surprise when Willie Labuschagne first described to me how

38

cheetah hunted ostrich in the Kalahari. These flightless birds can be anything up to 2,5 metres in height, and their legs are extremely powerful. A cheetah hunting an ostrich runs towards it at full speed. No stalking, no crouching. Just an attack. Although the ostrich runs hard (it can reach about 65 km an hour), the cheetah is soon within range and ready to strike. And it does this by flinging itself onto the side of the bird, holding on to one of its enormous wings which the ostrich holds open while in flight. The hunt is not over, because this does not bring the bird down yet. Instead, the ostrich literally drags the cheetah for some 80–100 metres, but its rate of stride is slowed down, until at last the cheetah manages to pull it over. It then takes the ostrich by its long neck, both mammal and bird twisting in the red Kalahari sand. The battle is fierce and the ostrich eventually succumbs. The cheetah's extreme agility enables it to keep out of range of those powerful legs (one blow from the leg of an ostrich means one severely injured cheetah), and on no occasion did Labuschagne see an ostrich inflict any injury on a cheetah. From hunting a hare one day, doing a high speed figure-of-eight, to being dragged by an ostrich the next day is, I think, fair evidence of this predator's adaptability.

Co-operative hunting between the individual cheetah of a group seldom occurs. Cheetah are solitary creatures by nature and as such are accustomed to hunting alone. There have been records of group hunting by cheetah but group co-operation does not take place on the scale that one encounters in the hunting methods employed by wild dogs or even lions. It is almost always the case that, even if more than one cheetah is present, only one individual will conduct the actual hunt, and no methodical co-operation takes place. Norman Myers witnessed a number of hunts end in failure, which he feels could have been

40

successful had concerted assistance been given by other nearby cheetah. Co-operative hunting between two species of carnivore is rare and if this does occur it probably evolves more by accident than design. There is a record of "co-operation" having been observed between a cheetah family and a group of black backed jackal in a number of hunting manoeuvres in the Nairobi National Park, and apparently this co-operation resulted in a higher rate of hunt success than was otherwise achieved. But such co-operation is very unusual, and I don't believe that this phenomenon is widespread, probably being confined to the particular individuals observed. Cheetah usually ignore jackals or else they simply chase them away.

The climax of a cheetah hunt is quick. The cheetah pursues its victim with lightning speed, and when it is close enough, strikes out with a forepaw, hitting the prey animal on the flank or rump, the dew claw causing a deep gash. This action throws the fleeing animal off balance, and the cheetah, holding it down with its forelegs and chest, quickly seizes it by the throat, the most common killing technique applied, or by the muzzle, taking care at the same time to remain out of range of the sharp kicking hooves of the struggling animal. Cheetah do not have the powerful jaws of the lion and the leopard, and their teeth are also much smaller than those of the larger predators, so they lack the equipment to kill other than by strangulation, or by "suffocation through a bite in the throat or around the muzzle". But the exact cause of the prey animal's death when the cheetah uses the throat bite is not always clear. The throat bite may, of course, result in the crushing of the windpipe, in which case death would be by strangulation. However, this is not always the case, for kills have been observed where the teeth of the cheetah entered the floor of the braincase of the prey animal. Death in these instances occurred very quickly, suggesting that it was not by strangulation that the animal died, but rather as a result of damage to the central nervous system. Certainly though, the cheetah is oriented toward a bite in the throat region of a prey animal and it is possible that the short canine teeth of cheetah, as opposed to the longer canines of the larger predators, preclude the cheetah from attacking any region other than the throat. I think a little caution is warranted when generalising on the cause of death of prey animals. With the larger ungulates, such as impala or Thomson's gazelle, the bite must be oriented to the throat region. But I do not think that this would necessarily apply to the smaller mammals cheetah prey on, such as the hare, which is small and has a relatively soft skin. The cheetah has to be extremely quick and agile when catching a hare, and if it happens to take it other than by the throat the canines may pierce vital internal organs which could cause death. In some cases, too, the neck vertebrae may be dislocated, even though the bite is from below and not from above, as in the case of a "neck" bite by other larger predators. Furthermore, cheetah have sharp and

laterally flattened canine teeth which in fact make for easy penetration between the vertebrae. Death of the prey animal may take in the region of 10 to 15 minutes, and the cheetah maintains its hold until the struggling animal lies still. The cheetah may release it at this stage but if the animal starts to struggle again, the cheetah will take it by the throat for several more minutes.

In hunting, a cheetah makes full use of its dew claw, once thought to be a functionless evolutionary left-over. These powerfully sharp and curved instruments are situated on the inside of each foreleg about ten cm above the top of the foot. The claw assists in overthrowing the prey animal and an account of the use of this weapon, dating back to 1885, illustrates this. In that year, Col. Julius Barras described the hunt of black buck with the aid of cheetah. On examining the carcass of a buck, he noticed a single, long deep gash on its flank. He was puzzled as to what had caused this wound, and then examined the cheetah, which was sitting on the cart. He writes: "I inspected it *(the cheetah)* closely and saw that the dew claw, which in the dog appears such a useless appendage, is represented in this brute by a terrible looking talon exactly suited to the infliction of such a gash."

Literature on the exact function of the cheetah's dew claw is scanty, and indeed, one gathers from the literature available that it is generally thought to be the blow of the cheetah's forepaw alone that is responsible for ending the flight of a prey animal. Col. R.W. Burton, in an effort to discover the exact function of the dew claws, approached K.S. Dharmakumarsinhji of Bhavnagar (India), who had had considerable experience in hunting with trained cheetah, and his comments were that the cheetah's main weapon of attack is the dew claw, without which it would be difficult for it to hold down large prey. "Our experience in hunting with cheetahs is that the dew claws are made full use of as hooks for holding onto black buck once the animal has been contacted.

Cheetahs with blunted dew claws were not able to control full sized black buck as effectively as those that possessed sharp, undamaged ones. We have found therefore that the dew claw is very important to the cheetah and he can also inflict a severe wound with it. Sometimes it is solely by means of the dew claws that the black buck is secured in the chase." It has also been suggested that because more often than not the swift blow by the cheetah's forepaw on the fleeing prey animal does leave a deep gash, it could be regarded as a pulling action on the part of the cheetah, rather than a striking blow which topples the prey. To my mind the sophisticated use of the forepaw is further evidence that this animal is a highly specialised and skilful hunter and stands apart from other felids in the wild.

After making a kill, a cheetah usually proceeds to move the carcass to the cover of a tree or a bush which offers shade. The carcass is dragged by the throat or nape and smaller prey may be carried by the head, neck, back or

rump. Exhausted after a fast run, the cheetah has to stop frequently whilst dragging its kill. Sometimes a cheetah drags its victim for a distance as great as 250 metres, but whether this is average or exceptional is difficult to say. The nature and availability of cover, I feel, is the deciding factor. When the cheetah has reached cover it does not begin to feed immediately, but rests for a while, panting from the exertion of the hunt. Should the predator be a female with very young cubs who are unable to make an incision through the tough hide of the carcass, the mother will do this first so that the cubs may begin to feed, but she herself will continue to rest.

Cheetah breathing rates have a wide range, from 16 breaths a minute for a cheetah lying resting in the shade to 156 breaths a minute for another cheetah after chasing and catching a juvenile warthog. The cheetah took 15 minutes to subdue the warthog and the high breathing rate was due probably to the protracted holding of the prey animal. A rate of 150 breaths a minute after a

200–300 metre chase has also been recorded. Eaton observed an adult cheetah, after an unsuccessful chase, stumble onto a steenbok, but the cheetah only pursued it "momentarily". He noticed that this cheetah's breathing rate appeared "very high" just prior to encountering the steenbok, and the winded condition evidenced by this high breathing rate probably precluded the cheetah from giving chase again.

There are two (and possibly more) reasons why a cheetah, once it has made a kill, proceeds to drag the carcass to some sort of cover, be it either a bush, a tree, or thick undergrowth. As seen from the breathing rates, it is clear that after an extensive chase the animal needs to recover from its exertions, and in order to do this it seeks out cover which will give it the required shade to facilitate recovery. This hypothesis is supported by the fact that even when a cheetah has been unsuccessful in bringing down a prey animal, it is winded after the chase and will seek shade, resting for a while before undertaking another hunt. A cheetah may also instinctively feel it necessary to conceal its kill, because of the danger of other predators being attracted either directly or through the give away activities of vultures, resulting in the possible loss of the cheetah's meal. Labuschagne told me that the cheetah in the Kalahari in most cases moved their kills to cover. If there was no cover available, the cheetah still moved the

carcass, and rarely ate where it had killed. It appears normal practice for a cheetah to drag or carry its prey away from where it has made a kill, whether cover is available or not. However, this does not always happen, and Lt. Col. Stevenson-Hamilton, first warden of the famous Kruger National Park, writes that prey in the Park is not dragged to cover, but is generally eaten where killed. Certainly this was the case with a cheetah kill which I saw in the Kruger National Park in 1970.

My husband and I watched a fully grown cheetah bring down an adult male impala one afternoon at about 5 p.m. The cheetah, with its victim, was about 100 metres from the side of the road, and although there was cover available in the form of bushes and trees, the cheetah did not in this instance drag the carcass to cover. I found this a little surprising at the time because in a matter of ten minutes the road was completely blocked with tourists' cars, and the cheetah appeared very nervous, enough to cause indigestion I should think. We watched this cheetah until just before 6 o'clock and decided to return early the following morning. We duly arrived at the spot to find the cheetah still there, although by this time fully gorged and looking a little uncomfortable with its distended belly. Vultures were assembled in the nearby trees and as impatience overtook them a few descended. The cheetah, rather half-heartedly at this stage

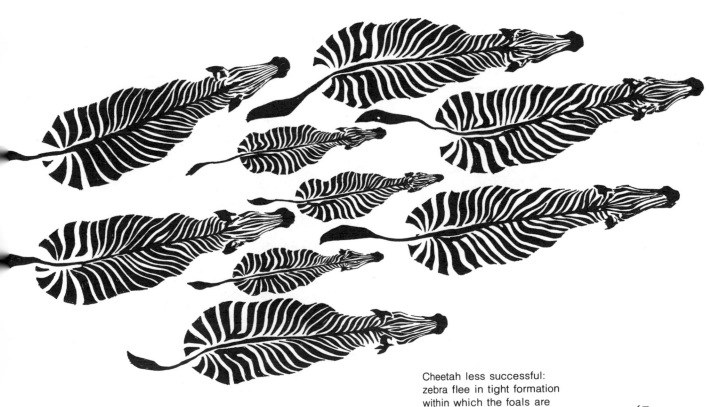

Cheetah less successful: zebra flee in tight formation within which the foals are protected

47

nuzzled the remains of the carcass a few times, and moved it first towards a tree and then behind a bush. Eventually the cheetah abandoned the remains and moved off.

The sudden descent of vultures from the sky when a kill is made acts as a signal to other predators in the area indicating the presence of food. Various predators (as well as tourists) have become "adept vulture watchers" moving off in the direction of the descending birds in search of the kill. George Schaller saw a female cheetah lose two kills, one to a lion and one to a hyaena, through this signalling effect of the vultures' descent. In most cases, vultures sit in nearby trees or on the ground waiting to scavenge the remains of a kill. But Schaller twice saw cheetah driven from their kills by a "solid phalanx of vultures". The cheetahs did little to retaliate, except to "hiss and moan in a

peculiar manner". However, in most cases, cheetah ignore the vultures, though on rare occasions they rush these birds "leaping into the air and swatting at an escaping one". In the incident in the Kruger National Park the presence of the vultures did not appear to upset the cheetah unduly even though it repeatedly glanced at them – it did seem that this cheetah had had enough to eat. This is certainly one cheetah that had a leisurely meal, instead of the usual rush, without being accosted by a variety of pilferers.

Cheetah, as with other predators, do not always have things their own way when hunting. It does happen that a cheetah fails to follow the sharp dodging action of a gazelle, and a cheetah has been seen to slip and fall while attempting a sharp turn. In the Kalahari, Labuschagne witnessed a cheetah chase a steenbok over three sand dunes for a distance of about 600 metres, and then give up.

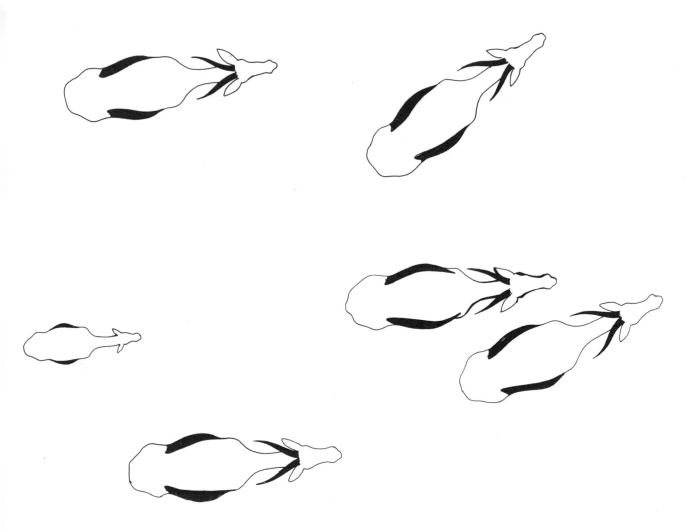

Cheetah more successful: Thomson's gazelle scatter when pursued

Apart from the "slip ups" which occur now and then, there are particular factors which limit the hunt of success of cheetah.

Large and concentrated herds of prey animals seem to confuse cheetah. Since a cheetah hunts by eyesight, it must be able to focus on one individual and pursue that individual when it takes flight. But a cheetah finds it difficult to fix on any one of the milling individuals in a large herd. Sometimes a cheetah may rush briefly at a herd of animals in order to scatter them and so isolate one. If this is successful, the cheetah will attempt an attack, but if the isolated individual mingles again with the rest of the herd, the predator does not pursue the matter. Lone animals or relatively small herds are probably more susceptible to attack since a cheetah will find it easier to focus its attention on one individual. Distance is another factor which may determine whether or not a hunt will be successful. From a relatively short range a cheetah stands a far better chance of bringing down a prey animal than were it to launch its attack from more than about 200–250 metres. And the greater the distance the more effort must the cheetah expend before reaching its prey. Dr R.F. Ewer makes an interesting statement to the effect that "the cheetah abandons any pursuit which might leave it exhausted when it finally came up with its quarry". This could indicate a realisation by the cheetah of the need for some reserve energy to subdue the captured prey.

Habitat? Adverse habitat conditions must surely affect the cheetah's hunt success. I have already mentioned that I consider the cheetah to be adaptable and flexible; it hunts in open grassland, it hunts in wooded areas, it hunts in arid and semi-arid areas. In this respect, the species is found over a wide range of varying habitats, and within each habitat it hunts successfully. But is it as successful in one habitat type as in another? Perhaps it is, although I tend to think that heavily bush encroached areas or forest are not acceptable to cheetah. But do we really know what *true* cheetah habitat is? Which is optimal for this animal? Which is marginal? And which is totally unacceptable? For an animal that runs down its prey, I am often told, open grassland is its true habitat. This though is not always the case. In the Serengeti the movements of cheetah are governed more by the movement of Thomson's gazelle than by vegetation. Cheetah in the Kafue National Park in Zambia do not hunt in the open grassland but instead confine themselves to the wooded areas. And Labuschagne tells me that he has seen cheetah "crashing through thorn-bush" after prey. A report in the Johannesburg *Sunday Times* of July 20, 1975 indicates that in the Hluhluwe and Umfolozi game reserves scientists have recently found that the cheetah, in thicker vegetation, succeeds in killing about 33% of the animals it attacks, whereas on the open plains this figure drops to 10%. I believe that cheetah *can* hunt in a variety of habitats, and the nature of true cheetah habitat is governed more by the availability of suitable prey animals than by vegetational composition. In any event I feel the many opinions and conclusions to be encountered emphasize the urgent need for studies to be initiated now, covering as many areas as possible, to establish whether any particular type of habitat is optimal for cheetah.

6 Predation

In spite of the work done on cheetah predation it is rather surprising how little we know about this aspect of cheetah ecology. To date there exists a limited number of publications and these are based mostly on short term field studies. Put these works together and the paucity of our knowledge is highlighted. Labuschagne studied cheetah in the Kruger National Park and in the Kalahari over a period of two years, the longest study of cheetah to date. Although his findings are not available at the time of writing this book, he has indicated to me that much of his information differs from other published works on this subject.

Predation should be viewed not only from the standpoint of the predator, such as what, when and how much it eats, it also embraces the effect of the predator on the different prey populations. It is one thing to say that the cheetahs' principal prey in East Africa appears to be the Thomson's gazelle but quite another to ask what impact cheetah predation has on this gazelle population. In an undisturbed ecosystem predator and prey populations actually complement one another. Under natural conditions, a predator usually kills according to its requirements and will rarely go on a slaughter spree, killing more than it can consume. Mass killing of prey has been reported on the odd occasion and in one particular incident a group of hyaena killed more than 110 Thomson's gazelle and maimed many others in one night. The hyaena ate little of what they had killed. If predators regularly undertook mass killing of prey animals they would very soon exhaust their own food supply, so such dramatic predator-prey interactions can be regarded as rare and isolated. Broadly speaking, predation could be described as having three different effects. It could be a limiting one, where the predator has a heavy impact on the prey population, or a regulatory one, where the predator and prey reach a form of balance. Or else, of course, the effect of a predator on a prey species may be negligible. The relationship between predator and prey is a delicate one, an intimate one. Watch a cheetah stalk, run and knock over its prey. A spectacular sight of which our understanding is superficial, because the kill has many hidden elements attached to it, some of which are known, some unknown.

A single sentence written by George Schaller constantly remains in my mind: "With different hunting patterns, each large carnivore fills a special niche." What niche does the cheetah fill? And what impact do cheetah have on prey animals in the different areas? To attempt to work out answers to these questions is a frustrating exercise, and unfortunately will remain so until, of course, we have more comprehensive information available. To elaborate. It has been estimated that the 200–250 cheetah in the Serengeti take approximately 16–21 000 Thomson's gazelle in a year. However, the estimated numbers of this particular prey species in the Serengeti range from 180 000 to 980 000.

This means that cheetah take anything from 2% to 11% of the existing gazelle population each year. At 2% the impact is negligible, at 11% it is major. So we don't really know.

Cheetah prey on a fairly wide variety of animals and the predation tables show the relative importance of each in the composition of those predation records available. But these figures should be considered in conjunction with a number of factors, such as seasonal distribution of prey species and the period over which the kills were observed. In some cases the relatively small sample figures given may not reflect a true pattern of predation by cheetah, and only long term observations would give a clearer picture. The greater proportion of prey animals fall into the small antelope, or the young of the larger antelope, category. Cheetah also prey on small mammals such as hare, springhare and antbear and where figures relative to these smaller mammals are low it should be remembered that the proportions are quite possibly underestimated due to the fact that the smaller mammals, in most cases, are rapidly and sometimes completely consumed. Consequently these kills are less frequently observed. Further, the absence of a carcass in those cases where smaller mammals are consumed entirely will surely bias predation records. So even the method by which kills are recorded, such as carcass returns or direct observations, may have a marked effect on the results obtained. When cheetah take small mammals very often no carcass is available, and a faecal analysis would be a possible method of assisting in the determination of dietary aspects of the predator-prey relationship. But this is no easy task, and Kruuk describes the results, and the difficulties in obtaining them, of the analysis of the faeces of the spotted hyaena. These results are extremely interesting, and such an analysis applied to cheetah faeces may bring forth more interesting information.

Cheetah appear to be influenced by a number of factors when they select prey animals. For example, the size of the prey, the vulnerability of the prey and the availability of the prey. Naturally, any one of these factors may act in conjunction with the others. A young fawn is both vulnerable and of the size category seemingly preferred by cheetah. Similarly, wildebeest calves fall into this size category, they are also vulnerable, and at calving seasons become available as a source of food. Larger prey animals may also be taken by cheetah, but this generally occurs only in those instances where a group of cheetah hunt together, which, it seems, does not often happen.

In East Africa, Thomson's gazelle appear to be the principal prey species of the cheetah. In the Serengeti certainly, the abundance and availability of the tommy throughout the year probably contributes to the cheetah's high rate of predation on this species. In fact George Schaller, who spent three years in the Serengeti, found that these gazelle were by far the most important food item in the cheetah's diet. Moreover, when the seasonal migration of these gazelle from the Seronera area to the Togoro plains takes place, the cheetah migrate with them. Normally cheetah are not found in the Togoro plains area but they do appear when the concentrations of the gazelle build up. The migratory habits of predators who follow prey animals on which they specialise is underlined by Walther who records that when wildebeest, zebra, buffalo or eland migrate to

11

12

11 Most of the day is spent resting

12 Or cheetah may take up an elevated position, possibly looking out for prey herds

13

14

13 A typical tree that
cheetah visit, one with
low slung and sloping
branches

14 Cheetah are not habitual
tree climbers, but they do
sometimes urinate or
defecate on low
branches

the Togoro area, cheetah do not follow, but lion do. Cheetah are invariably successful when hunting gazelle fawns, which are highly vulnerable due to their lack of speed and endurance. Actually Schaller's thirty-one observations of cheetah hunting fawns show that every single one was successful, "suggesting strong selection for that age class".

But the Serengeti cheetah do have a variation in their diet when the wildebeest calve, which happens almost exclusively on the plains during the months of January and February. There are more than 300 000 wildebeest in this area and they congregate in huge herds in the months of January and February, mostly in the central, eastern and southern areas. Over a four to six week period, practically all cows over the age of three years produce a calf and whereas Thomson's gazelle make up something like 75% of cheetah kills in the bush or mixed habitat, on the plains the proportion drops to about 40% due to the availability of the wildebeest calves. It becomes obvious how the reproductive seasons of some of the prey animals can have a rather dramatic effect on predation records.

Zebra (there are more than 200 000 in the Serengeti) drop their foals on the plains round about the same time as the wildebeest, but although the foals fall into the size category seemingly preferred by cheetah, they do not appear to be taken often. The escape tactics of a herd of zebra, which flees in tight formation (the foals are protected within the fleeing herd) probably prevent cheetah from following up an attack. Cheetah prefer to attack small scattered herds or isolated individuals, rather than large cohesive groups of animals. That rather formidable animal, the warthog, in spite of its relatively small size is not generally attacked by cheetah, and even lions are wary of this creature.

The predator-prey relationship between cheetah and reedbuck is an interesting one. Cheetah are an important predator on reedbuck in the Kruger National Park, having accounted for 22% of a total of 510 taken by all predators, over one study period. But in the Kafue National Park in Zambia, where reedbuck are more numerous, these small antelope are not an important prey species, even though they seem to favour an area that appears to be suitable cheetah habitat. In the Hluhluwe and Umfolozi Game Reserves in Zululand, South Africa, carcass returns of cheetah kills have shown a relatively high proportion of reedbuck, which in turn has given rise to some concern as the reedbuck population in Zululand is not, at the moment, what one might call prodigious. So here we have the apparent anomaly of the cheetah taking reedbuck in areas where this prey species is rare, and practically ignoring them where they are abundant. But so many factors, environmental, availability of other species and the like, can affect predator-prey relationships that perhaps there is in fact no anomaly at all. I fear we don't know enough about this relationship to assess what the situation actually is.

Just as the Thomson's gazelle in East Africa appear to be the principal prey species of cheetah, so in the Kruger National Park in South Africa, impala appear to be cheetahs' principal prey. These animals are the most abundant of cheetah prey species and Dr Pienaar lists them at 77% of all cheetah kills. But, although impala are numerous, in terms of prey preference they are rated only fifth in the diet of cheetah. At first, the term "prey preference" brought to my mind rather odd questions such as, does a predator actually prefer one species to another and does a predator methodically seek out one particular prey animal, ignoring others which are also prey species? Briefly, scientists in this particular field systematically work out the biomass of every species within a game reserve and these findings are then correlated with the kills made by any given predator. Pienaar's study indicates that reedbuck kills were not as numerous as impala kills, but carcass returns showed a higher rate of predation on these animals per unit of biomass than on impala. In terms of prey preference then, reedbuck rank higher than impala in the diet of cheetah.

Birds such as ostrich, guinea fowl, francolin and bustard are taken by cheetah although they do not appear in any great numbers in the predation records. There are two possible reasons for this. Either cheetah simply do not take many birds or, and I think this is the more probable, cheetah do take birds but no remains are found nor are the kills observed. Faecal analyses, could the difficulties be overcome, would perhaps indicate just to what extent birds do in fact make up part of a cheetah's diet.

In 1963 Bourlière postulated that carnivores prey on animals which are of about the same weight as themselves, and not on those which are much smaller or much larger than themselves. But from further information subsequently acquired from field research it appears that small mammals constitute quite a large proportion of the diet of a cheetah which hunts alone. The cheetah's preference for the smaller species of prey animals, weighing less than 60 kg, is in part probably related to the difficulty which cheetah may experience when trying to subdue the larger prey animals. But cheetah are at times successful in pulling down large prey such as puku, which can weigh up to 90 kg. These animals are abundant in the Kafue National Park in Zambia, and they comprise nearly half of the cheetah's diet. During the study period in this Park, of 15 puku taken, 8 were found to be adult. Although cheetah are not numerous in the Kafue Park, nearly the same number of puku are killed by cheetah as by leopard. And a further interesting point. Cheetah in the Kafue Park do not inhabit the extensive open plains, but rather the savannah woodlands, tree savannah and the smaller grasslands, which is the habitat preferred by the puku.

It seems that the physical condition of prey animals is not a major determining factor in the selection of prey by cheetah. Admittedly, old age and poor general physical condition of prey animals would make them vulnerable to predators because their reflex actions would not be as quick as the rest of a more healthy and robust herd. Such animals react in a manner not to their advantage, either fleeing at a slower pace than, or in a different direction to, the rest of the herd. This action immediately makes an animal vulnerable, and as the popular belief goes, predators are the "natural cullers" of debilitated animals. But does this apply to cheetah? Nearly all prey animals taken by cheetah in the Serengeti appeared to be healthy (99% of the total of 261 kills observed), the exceptions being two adult male Thomson's gazelle and a wildebeest which were infected with sarcoptic mange. Records from the Kafue National Park show that of cheetah prey, most were in the "good" condition class. The condition of the

15 A cheetah takes a prey
   animal
16 After subduing its prey,
   the cheetah pants from
   the exertion of the chase

East Africa:
Thomson's gazelle
and fawn

The principal prey species (in terms of numbers) taken by cheetah in certain regions of Southern Africa

58

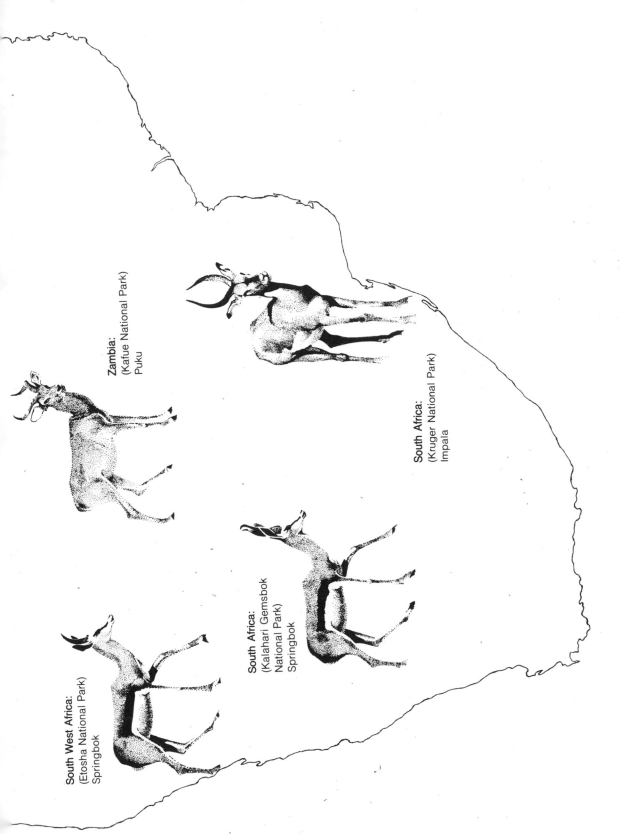

South West Africa:
(Etosha National Park)
Springbok

South Africa:
(Kalahari Gemsbok
National Park)
Springbok

Zambia:
(Kafue National Park)
Puku

South Africa:
(Kruger National Park)
Impala

59

prey animals was assessed, in most cases, from the state of the marrow in the femur, which is not an extremely reliable test, and therefore a true or sensitive picture is not obtained. Nevertheless the figures that emerge from studies in this Park as shown in Table III are interesting. Of 30 kills in the Nairobi National Park, only one prey animal was in poor physical condition.

These figures seem to indicate that the unexpected is true. Physical condition is not an important factor in the selection of prey animals. But if, as in the case of Kafue, the proportion of "poor" condition animals to "good" condition animals is very low, then perhaps the figures could indicate that animals in poor condition, when available, *are* taken in preference to others. Schaller speculates that perhaps the cheetah has the ability to assess the condition of the animal it is pursuing and to detect a physical weakness which may not be visible to the human eye. If this is valid, then cheetah may take more animals that are not in tip-top condition than is shown by analysis of carcasses as indicated in the predation records.

Large prey animals are sometimes taken, but this occurs only in those unusual cases where cheetah hunt in groups. In the Nairobi National Park cheetah killed kongoni and waterbuck and four adult cheetah successfully pulled down and killed an adult zebra. Two male cheetah killed a yearling topi weighing about 90 kg, but no strategic co-operation by individuals within a group was observed. A group of adult cheetah in the Nairobi National Park preyed heavily on waterbuck "which were abundant only in the locality in which they, as cubs, were reared" and Eaton remarks that the selection of waterbuck by these adults "became traditional, undoubtedly the result of learning and possibly a kind of imprinting". Eaton also mentions that cheetah experience difficulty in adapting to prey with which they are unfamiliar. Although this certainly is thought-provoking, I feel that more information over longer periods

Table III: *Condition of prey animals taken by predators in the Kafue National Park, Zambia*

| PREDATOR | CONDITION OF PREY ANIMALS | | | | NO. OF OBSERVATIONS |
	GOOD %	FAIR %	POOR %	TOTAL %	
Cheetah	66,6	22,2	11,1	99,9	9
Leopard	71,5	23,8	4,8	100,1	21
Lion	66,7	14,0	19,3	100,0	57
Wild dog	85,8	9,5	4,8	100,0	21

It has been said that few animals reach old age due to favourable hunting conditions, and prey animals are generally in good condition throughout the year. But note the small number of the cheetah observations. Six out of nine prey animals were in the "good" condition class. Had the results differed by only one in each age class, the percentages would have been very different.

of study is needed before we can say with any conviction that specialisation by cheetah on different prey species does, in fact, occur. The cheetah which were translocated from South West Africa to the Zululand game reserves are thriving in their new environment, and yet different prey species occur in these two areas. Thus, even if "imprinting" does occur, cheetah are sufficiently flexible to adapt to new prey species.

To obtain some insight into how often a cheetah kills, George Schaller, while in the Serengeti, kept a female cheetah and her two cubs, aged three to four months, under observation throughout the day for 26 days. She was not observed at night, but as she was usually located in the same area each morning, it was assumed that she had travelled very little, or not at all, during the night. The female confined herself to an area of ten square km of burnt grassland, the prey herds in this area consisting of Thomson's gazelle, Grant's gazelle and topi. During this period, the female killed 15 gazelle fawns, nine adult Thomson's gazelle and one hare. The total averaged about one kill a day. She failed to kill on three of the days, but on each of two days she killed two gazelle. Three kills were scavenged by lion and hyaena. At this rate of predation the female would average 337 gazelle kills in one year. Schaller then endeavoured to work out the actual food consumption of this female and her cubs. The average weight of an adult male gazelle is 16,5 kg and of an adult female 16,2 kg. Schaller visually estimated the weight of the fawns. From these figures he determined that the total weight of prey killed by this cheetah was 261,3 kg, an average of 10 kg a day, or 3 650 kg a year. Because parts of a carcass are not eaten (such as the digestive tract, and most of the bones and skin) and because three kills were scavenged by other predators, only 8,8 kg was available for actual consumption per day. Of this, 5,3 kg was consumed, the female eating about 4 kg a day and the cubs each about 0,5 kg.

Further observations of this same female some 18 months later, then accompanied by another litter of two cubs, showed that in nine days she killed five adult female Thomson's gazelle and two fawns. Another female cheetah, with a litter of three small cubs, was observed for six days, during which period she killed one gazelle on each of the six days. From yet further observations of female cheetahs with cubs, it emerges that they killed at the rate of about one gazelle a day. The killing frequency of a female cheetah with cubs is logically higher than that of solitary cheetah who kill approximately once every two to three days. It appears that a single cheetah in the Nairobi National Park will consume 10 to 12 kg at one time, which is quite a lot more than the Serengeti cheetah. Most of the figures for food consumption of cheetah in the wild, which scientists and field workers readily admit, are based on estimates. Schaller worked on an average weight of 16,5 kg for an adult male Thomson's gazelle, but I have heard that this animal can weigh up to 26 kg. As Schaller says, since this aspect of predation is based on several assumptions, these figures "are at best of the correct order of magnitude".

From the various records of adult cheetah in captivity, we find that they eat about 1 to 2 kg of red meat daily. Many captive cheetah are fed on whole, unplucked chickens, as it is considered by some that the feathers provide the

17

18

17 Cheetah normally drag the carcass to some sort of cover
18 Cheetah usually start feeding on the soft underparts of a prey animal
19 A typical feeding posture, using the carnassials to cut through the tough skin

20 The remains of a cheetah kill, in this instance a bushbuck. Cheetah do not eat even the smaller bones

21 Only the distal portions of the ribs are eaten

necessary roughage in their diet. Muscle meat, in itself, will not provide all the necessary nourishment, and in just about all the zoos and safari parks where cheetah are kept, the diet is supplemented with vitamin and mineral salts. Cod liver oil is also given to captive animals, but extreme care should be taken to ensure that the cod liver oil is *not* rancid, for this can induce the development of rickets, a disease of the skeleton. A point of interest here. Joy Adamson noticed mud-licking amongst the cheetah she observed, and says that by licking mud the cheetah obtain calcium and other minerals necessary for their diet. I made random enquiries about cheetah in captivity and established that at De Wildt Estates the cheetah were observed licking mud when they were under one year old. But they stopped this activity when they became older. At the time they were observed licking mud their diet of chicken and red meat was not being supplemented by vitamins and minerals.

Cheetah, when feeding on a carcass that is lying on its side, will characteristically eat the meat off the upper flank, hind, forequarter and spine before turning it over. The distal portions of the ribs and cartilage are also eaten. Most popular portions are the heart, kidneys, liver, milt, trachea, ventral part of the jaw and the eyes. Sometimes cheetah eat the gall bladder by mistake, which Labuschagne has told me, is very small and easily overlooked, and this causes them to vomit. Cheetah avoid the intestines, although Joy Adamson describes Pippa of *Spotted Sphinx* fame as eating the intestines in "spaghetti like fashion". The stomach and the intestines are sometimes dragged from the carcass to one side, but these soft parts are not buried or even covered with soil. Blood that collects in the body cavity is lapped up which is a "useful behaviour in a predator that inhabits semi-desert country in which water is often scarce," writes Schaller. All that remains of the larger kills is a skeleton with most of the skin attached and the digestive tract. Dr C.K. Brain, who carried out feeding experiments with five cheetah in South West Africa, came to a similar conclusion as a result of his observations. When cheetah were fed a springbok, almost the whole of the skeleton and the skin was left behind. Cheetah, because of their smaller teeth, are restricted to eating the soft and "fragile" parts of the skeleton of a prey animal, such as the ribs, vertebral process and the scapula. However, when the cheetah were fed a baboon a different feeding pattern emerged. Because of the "less robust" structure of the skeleton of a baboon compared to that of the springbok, the cheetah were able to eat the whole of the vertebral column, the hands and feet, as well as the ends of the limb bones.

Cheetah eat very rapidly and occasionally stop to glance about, giving the impression of being nervous. A friend of mine, who watched two adult cheetah feeding on an impala carcass in the Kruger National Park, said he thought the animals would never finish as they spent so much time glancing over their shoulders. But it does happen that a cheetah's kill will be expropriated by other predators such as lion, leopard and hyaena and in the Serengeti 20 out of 238 kills were taken by lion, 11 by hyaena and one by leopard, a 13% loss. It is therefore to the cheetah's advantage to eat rapidly and as much as it can before the possible arrival of other predators.

The length of time cheetah spend on a carcass varies considerably. No

Threat posture

Black cub in the Kalahari. Even at this young age the cub knows how to spit and hiss

doubt the size of the carcass and the number of cheetah feeding on it are important considerations. An adult female with two cubs was recorded to take from 50 to 120 minutes to finish an adult gazelle. Feeding times by more than one adult cheetah on the carcass of young fawns average 15 to 35 minutes, and an adult female with cubs requires about 70 minutes to consume a fawn. Noteworthy here is the fact that cheetah have no means of storing and ensuring the safety of a kill. Lion, in some areas, often remain at a kill for quite a time, and their very presence safeguards the carcass for later feeding. Leopard store kills in trees out of the reach of scavengers and other predators, and hyaena cache their food in water. But the cheetah has no larder and must deal with its kill in one sitting.

Very little information exists on cheetahs' water requirements. Cheetah in the Seronera area of the Serengeti drink water at irregular intervals at the river in the daytime and at night. Labuschagne has told me that the water requirements of cheetah in the Kalahari is not a factor which governs their movements and they go without water for about ten days or longer. He twice observed cheetah eating tsama melon, which has a high water content.

Cheetah are not carrion eaters. True enough, there have been exceptions, but only of a few cheetah. I was therefore a bit surprised to read that cheetah "will feed readily from carrion", but unfortunately the authors of the publication give no specific examples. The exceptions regarding carrion emanate from the Kruger National Park where, during the anthrax epidemic of 1960-61 a "few cheetah" fed on carcasses that were infected with anthrax, subsequently contracting the disease which led to their death. In 1964 a cheetah was seen eating from the carcass of a buffalo which had been killed by lions a few days before. These cheetah, Dr Pienaar told me, were not disabled in any way, but had most probably been unsuccessful in their hunting for some time and were driven through hunger to feed on these carcasses. A cheetah in captivity is not averse to feeding on an animal that it has not killed itself, providing the meat is not very high, that it is not, in fact, carrion.

Table IV: *Composition of cheetah prey in the Serengeti National Park (Schaller 1968; 1972)*
261 kills, comprising nine species of prey animals

PREY SPECIES	NUMBER OF KILLS	%
Thomson's gazelle	238	91,2
Grant's gazelle	6	2,3
Reedbuck	2	0,8
Wildebeest	5	1,9
Topi	2	0,8
Hartebeest	1	0,4
Dik-dik	1	0,4
Impala	3	1,1
Hare	3	1,1
Nine prey species	261	100,0

Table V: *Composition of cheetah prey in the Serengeti National Park (Kruuk and Turner 1967)*
23 kills, comprising five species of prey animals

PREY SPECIES	NUMBER OF KILLS	%
Thomson's gazelle (adult)	12	52
Wildebeest (juvenile)	5	22
Kongoni (juvenile)	1	4
Wildebeest	1	4
Kongoni	1	4
Zebra (yearling)	1	4
Hare	1	4
Thomson's gazelle (juvenile)	1	4
Five prey species	23	98

Table VI: *Composition of cheetah prey in East Africa (Graham 1966)*
173 kills, comprising 25 species of prey animals (information from 205
people via interviews and questionnaires)

PREY SPECIES	NUMBER OF KILLS	%
Thomson's gazelle	38	22,0
Grant's gazelle	37	21,4
Impala	27	15,6
Oribi	7 }	8,1
Hare	7	
Wildebeest	6	3,5
Coke's hartebeest	5 }	5,8
Gerenuk	5	
Burchell's zebra	4	
Steenbok	4 }	6,9
Ostrich	4	
Oryx	3	
Dik-dik	3	
Topi	3	
Waterbuck	3 }	10,4
Warthog	3	
Guinea fowl	3	
Lesser kudu	2	
Bushbuck	2 }	3,5
Greater bustard	2	
Grevy's zebra	1	
Roan antelope	1	
Duiker	1 }	2,8
Jackal	1	
Molerat	1	
25 prey species	173	100,0

Sex ratio of adults – Males: 25
Females: 13
Not sexed: 92

Table VII: *Composition of cheetah prey in the Kafue National Park (Mitchell et al., 1965)*

33 kills, comprising eleven species of prey animals

PREY SPECIES	NUMBER OF KILLS	%
Puku	15	45,5
Reedbuck	4	12,0
Hartebeest	3	9,1
Impala	2	
Warthog	2	
Wildebeest (1 calf; 1 unknown)	2	18,2
Bushbuck	1	
Duiker	1	
Kudu (young prime)	1	
Oribi (calf)	1	15,2
Zebra (foal)	1	
Eleven prey species	33	100,0

Table VIII: *Composition of cheetah prey in the Kruger National Park (Pienaar 1969)*

152 carcass returns, comprising approximately ten species of prey animals, for the period Feb. 1966 to Jan. 1968

PREY SPECIES	NUMBER OF KILLS	%
Impala	104	68,43
Waterbuck (suckling young and juveniles)	17	11,18
Zebra (foals)	2	1,32
Wildebeest (unknown)	1	0,66
Kudu (young and juvenile)	7	4,60
Warthog	1	0,66
Reedbuck	9	5,92
Duiker	4	2,63
Others	7	4,60
Approx. ten prey species	152	100,00

Table XI: *Composition of cheetah prey in the Timbavati Private Nature Reserve (Hirst 1969; Hall-Martin, pers. comm.) 50 kills, comprising five species of prey animals*

PREY SPECIES*	NUMBER OF KILLS	%
Impala	41	82
Wildebeest	3	6
Kudu	4	8
Zebra (foal)	1	2
Steenbok	1	2
Five prey species	50	100

*Animals from all age classes were taken

7 Social Structure

Cheetah are not gregarious, they seldom *form* groups, and those groups that exist generally consist of a mother with cubs, or of a litter from which the mother has taken her leave. The solitary cheetah is certainly not an oddity, and some writers maintain that cheetah normally live alone. Although the results of a study in one area indicate that groups of cheetah appear to be common, a study in another area reveals a prevalence of solitary cheetah. Why this variation? I pondered this question one day as I sat near a young female cheetah. The sleek cat gave away no secrets, with calm and enigmatic aloofness she no more than tolerated my presence.

Adult cheetah are mostly solitary, although in the Kruger National Park and the Nairobi National Park cheetah are often encountered in pairs or in mother-cub groups. In the Serengeti, of a sample of 244 cheetah unaccompanied by cubs, 52% were solitary, 31% were in groups of two, 14% in groups of three and 3% in groups of four. Of 1 794 adult cheetah in East Africa, 27% were found to be solitary, 34% were in groups of two, 19% in groups of three and 20% in groups of four to 12 animals. Cheetah in Botswana are normally found in pairs or family groups and they are also sometimes found singly.

Adult females do not form groups, but adult males sometimes do link up, although not necessarily on a permanent basis. Other than those composed of adult males, all groups encountered by Schaller in the Serengeti were litter mates that had broken away from their mothers. Some of these were of mixed sexes and others young of the same sex. Prior to a female cheetah coming into oestrus for the first time she takes leave of her brothers and sisters and goes off on her own, and the males may, or may not, stay together as a group. In the Nairobi National Park, over a period of some four months, Eaton studied four groups of cheetah, each of which had a differing social structure. One group consisted of three males and two females, one of two males (known litter mates), another of two males and one female and the fourth of a female with cubs. Eaton believes that each of these groups had a leader, and the leader was a male, except for the group of the female with cubs, where the adult female was the leader. But parental care may be a more apt description of this female's activity, rather than leadership. Eaton doubts if the leader is socially dominant, and it is not known how leadership is established. In a subsequent study in this Park, McLaughlin records no groups composed of adult male and female cheetah. This gives me the impression that cheetah group structure is fluid, and is very likely to change according to the conditions prevailing at any given time. Even although groups of cheetah have been reported, the only consistent group composition seems to be that of a female with her growing cubs, and that of litter mates.

A female with cubs avoids any form of social contact with other cheetah

22 Very little is known about the social structure of cheetah

groups. They never associate with other adult cheetah, nor do they associate with the grown cubs from a previous litter. Although visual encounters may occur between a female with cubs and other cheetah the female is generally respected and the other cheetah will not interfere with her.

And yet family groups comprising both adult and young cheetah have been reported. Results of an East African survey show that 37% of litters were accompanied by more than one adult. And in the Kruger National Park, although some solitary animals were sighted, cheetah occur mainly in groups, either pairs or family groups of up to eight in number. It has been mentioned that family groups, "father, mother and one or two large cubs" are not uncommon in East Africa. Nevertheless, I could nowhere find any literature which dealt with the role of the other adult, or adults, in relation to the mother and her cubs, and in fact, although family groups have been reported the relationship to the cubs of any additional adults in a group is unknown. In this context, Eaton comments that where a litter is observed with more than one adult present, rather than a second parental animal, the additional cheetah is probably a male following an oestrous female.

Although there are cases where cheetah are seen together, and from this it is sometimes construed that cheetah are not solitary creatures, one should be careful of generalizations based on the results of studies in only one or two different areas. Furthermore, there are times when two males may join up for a few days on a casual basis only to separate again later, each one going its own way. Also, there is an identification difficulty which arises when a female cheetah is accompanied by her nearly fully grown cubs. And this point is emphasised by Schaller, who encountered one female with four large cubs and another with five large cubs, all of which, he says, would have been classed as adults by casual observation. It should also be remembered that when the cubs are mature, the mother will take leave and quite often the litter mates stay together for some time. And, as indicated earlier, females of the litter may remain with the group until their first oestrous period. There is then the distinct possibility that, from an encounter with a group of nearly fully grown cubs, the conviction that cheetah normally live in groups can arise. But over a period of time it is probable that this group of animals will split up. A friend of mine exclaimed that cheetah are most definitely not solitary because he once saw two cheetah together. Well, first I asked if they were young animals likely to be litter mates, and then I asked if they were a female and a fully grown cub. He couldn't say, which is indicative of the problem that faces most of us when trying to classify cheetah.

Published literature comes to no conclusions regarding the significance of sex ratios in cheetah populations, nor is it anywhere indicated what proportions of males and females constitute a healthy and productive population. In vertebrates, the sex ratio at birth is more or less 50-50 but by the time these animals are mature this ratio may have changed to favour either male or female, depending on various aspects such as the species, the habitat or mortality. Zebra may experience just this sort of trend, because the zebra males, when a herd is in flight, take up a position in the rear, and are thus more susceptible to predation.

The adult male to female ratio of cheetah in the Serengeti is 1 : 2, and Schaller gives the population of this area as 21% males, 47% females, and 32% young. He points out that it was difficult to obtain an unbiased ratio since the accurate counting of cheetah is well nigh impossible. In East Africa 47 adults were sexed, and 39 were found to be males and eight were females. However, these latter figures were drawn from the results of a survey based largely on questionnaires and interviews of some 200 people, and I feel should be evaluated with a certain amount of caution. We come back to the identification problem again, and there is a strong possibility that some of the adult cheetah observed may not have been accurately sexed.

In the Kruger National Park during the predator control campaign which ended in 1960, 51 cheetah were sexed after being destroyed and of these, 69% were males and 31% were females. Subsequent to this campaign, 471 live cheetah were sexed and 58% were found to be males and 42% were females. From these figures it becomes clear that the overall sex ratio of the population in the Kruger National Park at that time favoured males. The figure of 471 "live" cheetah is somewhat misleading to the layman and could give rise to the idea that there are at least 471 cheetah in the Kruger National Park (actually the numbers fluctuate around the 250 mark). The figure of 471 can not be interpreted as an actual number of cheetah in the Park, but represents the sexing of cheetah over a protracted period according to the grid system of recording. This system is designed to produce a ratio and not absolute numbers.

It may be significant that in the Serengeti more females than males were recorded, while in the Kruger National Park the opposite was the case. However, the significance (if any) remains obscure. A variety of "reasons" for the different sex ratios could be put forward, such as for example, perhaps in the Serengeti cheetah males are more susceptible than females to disease and mortality. But without evidence and with no factual knowledge available, such thinking although interesting, is extremely speculative.

Regarding the sex ratios of cheetah cubs, no evaluations concerning trends appear to exist, and undoubtedly information on this subject would be extremely difficult to gather. In the Serengeti, Schaller sexed five litters of black cubs (up to three months old), and found that there were four males and seven females, but he points out that these were the surviving cubs of the particular litters, some already having "disappeared". A further 14 litters of "small to large cubs" were sexed and this revealed ten males and 18 females, making overall totals of cubs sexed of 14 males and 25 females. Records of cubs sexed in the Nairobi National Park show nine males and two females. On the whole, captive litters have, to date, shown no bias towards male or female cubs (see Appendix V). But this can vary as, of five captive litters produced at Whipsnade Park in England, four cubs were males and eight were females. At Montpellier Park in France where four captive litters were born, the opposite was the case, as, of the total number of cubs born, nine were males and six were females.

Predators generally produce several young at a time, in contrast to most herbivores which produce only one offspring during a breeding season. Further, felids are usually polyoestrus so that the female is capable of producing a second litter almost immediately should she lose the first. Cheetah, amongst the larger cats, show a tendency to produce, at times, rather larger litters than do the other big cats. George Schaller has said that leopard produce an average of two young at a time and lions produce 2 to 2,5. Why do cheetah produce more offspring than lion or leopard? Perhaps this has something to do with the fact that cheetah face more critical pressures militating against their survival than do the other predators and so, as a kind of insurance, more cubs are born. Cub mortality amongst cheetah is high and larger litters may be a "built-in safety mechanism to safe-guard cheetah against any critical pressures" writes Norman Myers. But how well this safety mechanism actually works is open to question.

Various cheetah litter sizes have been observed and these exhibit a fairly wide range of difference. Perhaps the differences are related to environmental conditions, for most of the records of births in captivity seem to indicate a smaller litter size than for births in the wild. But consider – during the predator control period in the Kruger National Park mentioned earlier, lions were shot in great numbers, whereupon the numbers of lion cubs per litter promptly rose from the usual two or three to five or six. When the programme ended, litter sizes dropped back to the previous level. It seems that the lions regulated their litter sizes according to their population numbers in relation to their environment, in which ample prey was available. Would this phenomenon occur within a cheetah community? Would cheetah, when their numbers are low (how little is "low"?) increase their litter size? Conversely, in an area where cheetah numbers are high (and how many is "high"?), would litter sizes tend to be smaller?

And now a further complication enters the picture. The number of cubs in a litter show a tendency to drop as the litter grows older. Mortality among small

Table X: *Litter Sizes*

LOCALITY	RANGE OF LITTER SIZES	REFERENCE
Wild:		
East Africa	of 16 litters, 6 had 4 cubs each and 3 had 8 cubs each	Graham & Parker (1965)
East Africa	3-6 (sample of 6 litters)	McLaughlin (1970)
East Africa	usually 5	Eaton (1971)
East Africa	at least 4	Eaton (1970)
East Africa	average 3-4 (sample of 14 litters)	Schaller (1972)
East Africa	1-6	Adamson (1972)
South Africa	2-5	Pienaar (1963)
Captive:		
Philadelphia Zoo, U.S.A.	3,2	Ulmer (1957)
Krefeld Zoo, Germany	4	Encke (1961)
Whipsnade Park, England	3,3,2,3,1	Manton (1970, 1971)
Montpellier Park, France	3,4,4,4	Vallat (pers.comm.)
Beekse Bergen Park, Holland	5,5	Tong (pers.comm.)

23 Grooming does take place, sometimes quite frequently, but not with the intensiveness that one finds in other animal species

cubs is high (in East Africa only about 50% of cubs survive), so the age of the cubs when the litter size is recorded is important to the consideration of litter sizes *at birth*. There is then the possibility that available information on litter sizes in the wild may not be strictly applicable to the numbers of cubs actually born.

Before discussing territory and home range as it may or may not apply to cheetah, it is as well to examine briefly these two concepts, as both terms are rather loosely used. The concept of territory is not a new one, but it is only within the last few decades that much attention has been given this by scientists. Territoriality, it has been said, is "a fundamental characteristic of animals in general". However this does not necessarily mean that the characteristic is found in all animals, or that it is developed to the same degree. There are many definitions used to describe territory of different species under varying circumstances, but basically any defended area is regarded as a territory. The home range, the size of which will depend on the kind of animal, its requirements, sex, age (possibly) and the seasons (some animals are migratory), "is the area, usually around a home site, over which the animal normally travels in search of food".

Very little information exists on these two concepts as they apply to cheetah. In fact no detailed scientific study (except that by Labuschagne) has been undertaken to establish whether cheetah are territorial or not and to what extent a home range may or may not exist. Schaller mentions that cheetah are not territorial, and says that on the Serengeti plains they follow the movements of the Thomson's gazelle, their principal prey animal. He implies that their territory is not fixed, and that contact with others is avoided by means of scent and smell; cheetah faeces are an integral part of the marking system and are never covered with soil. He also mentions that "land tenure" systems are affected by local environmental conditions, and one cannot state as general behaviour any particular form of territoriality which has been observed in any specific instance. He observed adult cheetah watch each other on several occasions at distances of 200 to 600 metres, and each maintained its position, neither advancing nor retreating. He also observed a mother and her daughters, each with a litter, hunt in the same area for a few weeks, and although they saw each other, to his knowledge they never associated.

Eaton says that the cheetah groups he studied in the Nairobi National Park employed a spacing system technique that works on a "time-plan" which he advocates is a special type of territoriality. Time-plan is basically a system of avoidance. When one cheetah group comes across the fresh (less than 24 hours old) markings of another group, the cheetah smell the marking and move off. Should the marking be more than 24 hours old it is not respected. Territories are thus allowed to overlap, but the marking system ensures that different cheetah groups do not frequent the same specific area at the same time. McLaughlin mentions that the ranges of the groups which he studied, also in the Nairobi National Park, overlapped extensively but the scent markings were inefficient in that to a large extent they were disregarded. He concludes from this that cheetah are probably not territorially inclined.

From the Kalahari Gemsbok National Park in the northern Cape Province quite a different pattern emerges from the study undertaken by Labuschagne, who spent one year in that vast, undulating area. He classified cheetah under three possible categories. First is the female with her cubs, which he has termed *temporarily territorial,* or those animals possessing a home range. The female, says Labuschagne, is territorial only for the period that she is raising her young family. The second category is the *nomad.* This animal ignores boundary markings and travels in a more or less specific direction. And the third category is the animal that is *strictly territorial.* Large overlap of territory does occur, but the territorial animal will actively defend an area against any intruder should actual confrontation take place. A cheetah's territory is, I should imagine, a large one, and to defend it, at all times, would be impossible. The time spent pacing the boundary of a large territory and marking it would leave no time at all for food or females. But woe betide the nomad who ignores a boundary and walks into a territorial male for he is likely to have the spots knocked off him. Labuschagne says that when a cheetah makes close contact with a territorial animal, ferocious fighting occurs.

Very few cases of aggression between cheetah have been recorded in the wild, and those of only a minor nature. But two cases of direct aggression in the Kruger National Park each resulted in one male killing another. In neither case is it known whether the conflict was over territory, a carcass or the rights to a female. In one case, two cheetah were observed fighting in a clearing one evening near the Crocodile River. The following morning a ranger went out to the spot and found a dead male cheetah, which had a portion of its neck and shoulder eaten away. Close by lay a reedbuck ram, which was untouched. In the other instance, near Shingwedzi, a large male cheetah was observed to kill and partially devour another cheetah. Stevenson-Hamilton indicates that perhaps in these reported cases of cannibalism, which he says is "quite common among chitas", two males have either fought over a kill or for possession of a female, and the struggle combined with the taste of blood would lead the victor, whilst still "under the influence of excitement", subconsciously to follow his instinct of devouring what he has killed. He concludes "but all the cat, unlike the dog tribe, are more or less addicted to cannibalism, quite irrespective of their being possessed by hunger".

The social structure of cheetah is not a stable one, nor does it follow a pattern from one area to another. These animals are variously termed solitary, social, territorial and non-territorial. It seems that no broad or general statements can be made regarding many aspects of the cheetah's life style. But the overall impression gained from the various works done on this aspect is that cheetah are territorial. I also think that these animals are sufficiently capable and flexible enough to modify this basic characteristic in relation to the density of cheetah populations from one area to another.

8 The Process of Reproduction

Imagine for a moment that you are holding a cheetah cub. Its softness and warmth tempt you to cuddle this little creature, but a sudden sharp hiss warns you that though small, this *is* a wild animal. This cub, a result of the fusion of two cells, is evidence that life perpetuates life, a part of the reproductive process which occurs in all life forms however different in appearance. Certain ritualistic behaviour patterns and specific responses are sometimes essential to the fruitful culmination of courtship between the male and the female of most species of mammals and birds. An interruption of this process can mean that mating will not result in fertilisation, or that mating will not take place at all. If the pattern is broken, if either male or female does not respond to the often specialised ritualistic behaviour of the other, the fusion of cells will not occur, and the cub you are holding remains imaginary.

Some initial elements are identifiable in the function of courtship. An initial stimulus of a behavioural, vocal or olfactory nature attracts a male to a female, or vice versa. Usually both male and female exhibit courtship behaviour patterns, and one of the functions of courtship is to release sexual responses in the animals by way of specific signals. As the courtship progresses, male and female become attuned to each other's behaviour, and this culminates in the breeding pair mating. For instance, the action (called *lordosis*) of the female in presenting herself by crouching down low will stimulate the male to mount her, but if the female moves away when the male approaches, he will be discouraged. We can therefore understand that every movement, action or signal by one or the other is part of the process of reproductive behaviour which sexually motivates a breeding pair.

Few observations have been made, in the wild, of the courtship behaviour of cheetah, so most of our knowledge stems from the study of cheetah in captivity. We do gain some insight into the reproductive behaviour of these animals from the correlation of available literature relative to the studies and observations of this particular aspect. From this, a pattern emerges and it becomes clear that cheetah courtship is highly specialised. It is, in fact, a typical felid courtship where the female, initially, when the male approaches her, spits at him with a "how dare you touch me" attitude, and any attempt by the male to establish physical contact is met with great indignation by the female. But as the courtship progresses, a change takes place. The female begins to entice the male and uses all her womanly wiles to maintain his interest.

It is as well at this point to describe in broad outline some of the characteristics of the female reproductive cycle. For simplicity of discussion, each cycle can be described as consisting of three phases, pro-oestrus, oestrus and met-oestrus. Each cycle lasts approximately seven to fourteen days although I feel that this may vary with individuals and the conditions under which they live. In one captive female, oestrus (or cycle) lasted about fifteen days, with an inter-oestrous period of about seven to ten days. If fertilisation does not take place, the female will cycle again, perhaps two or three times. Re-cycling may occur within three to five days, but again this can vary. Ann van Dyk tells me that the re-cycling by two of the females at De Wildt Estates seemed to take place at ten day intervals, with a cycle lasting about five days. It is not always easy to establish oestrus in a female cheetah. The vaginal discharge is not always apparent, and although the vagina may in some instances become swollen, this is not always visible. Some captive females have shown a slight vaginal bleeding during pro-oestrus, but possibly a much safer method of determining this condition is a study of the behaviour of these animals.

In the wild a female does not associate with other cheetah, but when she comes into season she leaves a scent trail, which males can follow, through the discharge of sex hormones in her urine. Several males will mate with the female over a number of days. To simulate these breeding conditions in captivity, a pre-requisite seems to be the separation of the males and female throughout the year, and the introduction of two or even three males to a female only when

Female and male response chart[1]

CYCLE	FEMALE	MALE
	Interaction minimal Start of courtship	
PRO-OESTRUS (1st phase)	Vaginal discharge (not always visible) Stutter call Rolling?	Smelling of the vagina Stutter call Erections and spraying Mound building? Charging at the female
	Non-receptive and swats at approaching males	Inter-male aggression
OESTRUS[2] (2nd phase)	Receptive Lateral tail displacement Copulation (infrequent)	Male aggression reaches peak Partial mounting
MET-OESTRUS (3rd phase)	Hormonal change Interest minimal Courtship ceases[3]	Aggression minimal

1: This chart is derived from observations of certain captive animals.
2: Most carnivores are induced ovulators, which means that the females will ovulate when actual mating takes place. But it is not clear if cheetah ovulate freely during the second phase of the cycle, or if liberation of the ova occurs only when copulation takes place.
3: If fertilisation does not occur, the female will, within about 10 days, start another cycle.

79

24

25

24 A male cheetah squirting urine, which is a means of marking. Johan Degenaar has found that at times some female cheetah adopt a similar posture when urinating

25 A typical mound onto which a cheetah has defecated. Mound building by male cheetah may possibly increase in frequency when a female is in oestrus.

Mating posture

A close up of the mating posture, showing the neck bite. These two photographs were taken at the Varadays' Cheetah Sanctuary near Loskop Dam in the Transvaal

This captive female produced five cubs in December 1974 at Collisheen Estates in Natal, much to the delight of Neil Hulett on whose property the animals live

she is in oestrus*. If cheetah in captivity continually share an encampment, they will probably not mate. A sexual anxiety between males and female must be created at breeding times but if the animals live together all year then no such anxiety arises.

An increase in activity among the captive animals will usually begin some two to three weeks before a female starts her cycle. Vocalisation, a distinct *stutter* call, between males and female is frequently heard and some aggression in the form of brief and minor scuffles occurs. The frequency of spraying (a means of marking) by the sexually motivated males increases, and mound building, possibly another form of marking, has also been observed. The male cheetah does this simply by building a small mound of earth with his hind legs, and urinating or defecating on top of it. These mounds, which are not covered with soil, may be a means of communicating with a female in oestrus. The building of mounds is not confined only to breeding times, and I have seen a number of small earth mounds onto which a cheetah had defecated, but this activity may increase significantly in frequency when a female is in oestrus.

In general, it seems that two or more males should be released into the female's encampment when signs of oestrus are noticed. The introduction of more than one male to a female's enclosure is important. The males become aggressive towards one another which is essential for the sexual arousal of the female. Count Spinelli who has successfully bred cheetah in captivity at his private zoo just outside Rome, believes that more than one male with an oestrous female is more likely to induce successful mating than if only a single male is present. On two occasions, when his captive female was in oestrus, Spinelli borrowed two males from the Rome Zoo, for mating. When the males were introduced to the female for the first time, she became agitated and whenever the males approached her she "stood in a defensive position". At Whipsnade Park in England this same form of aggressiveness was present when a male was released into the female's enclosure. She was extremely agitated even to the extent of trying to climb out of the enclosure. The male inflicted one or two minor skin cuts on the female, but nothing serious enough to warrant interference by the Park authorities. In both instances, the initial aggressiveness progressed to the animals becoming more agreeable to each other. This aggression is an important and necessary element of the courtship. George Schaller mentions an instance in the Serengeti when he saw two males "briefly rear up and slap each other" as a female stood nearby watching. This may well have been a part of the reproductive process.

Dr Robert Herdman, ethologist attached to the San Diego Zoological Society in the United States, has for some years closely studied the problems concerning the reproductive behaviour of captive cheetah. From his observations, Dr Herdman says it became "increasingly obvious that male interaction to females is most important". He feels that the introduction of

*Conditions under which cheetah have bred in captivity vary considerably; for a detailed report on this matter refer to Thompson and Vestal (1974)

males may induce pro-oestrus in the female, and inter-male aggression during courtship is important to stimulate the release of sufficient hormones in the female to cause ovulation. A further interesting point mentioned by Herdman concerns the vaginal smears which were taken from a captive female who had not been in contact with males. These tests were done every week for a year, and the results showed that this female (whose age I could not establish, unfortunately) had not cycled. Without the presence of a male, no behaviour indicating oestrus took place. This is in sharp contrast to other captive females. Count Spinelli's female cheetah cycled regularly, without the presence of males.

During the pro-oestrus phase of the cycle the actual courtship begins. The stutter call, which assisted in the making of contact between male and female has served its purpose, and now an aggressiveness arises between male and female. The males charge the female and she in turn retaliates. The female, of course, is not yet receptive and when the males approach her for the purpose of testing her responsiveness, she lies down and spits and swats at them. The frequency of urinal spraying by the males increases and inter-male aggression breaks out. These activities are carefully watched by the female and are important in urging her into true oestrus. Without this atmosphere the essential reproductive hormonal change will not take place in the female's system. Inter-male aggression soon reaches its peak and the dominant male establishes himself. It is at this point, in captivity, that "male management" should be practised, says Dr Herdman, whose observations revealed that male to male aggression was important in arousing the female but continuing male aggression may displace sexual interest in the female and also interfere with copulation. He suggests that when the female is sufficiently aroused and entering oestrus, the subordinate male should be removed, and the breeding pair left alone. A contrasting tenet is followed at the Lion Country Safari Parks also in America where as many as six males are left with one female throughout the entire process.

As the courtship progresses, the behaviour of the breeding animals undergoes a change. Initially a process of orientation of one to the other took place. Thereafter aggression occurred between competing males (and a lesser aggression between males and female) which in fact served to stimulate release of the female's reproductive hormones. The female then allows the males to approach her, and her behaviour is not one of discouragement as witnessed in the first phase of the cycle. To complete the courtship, certain behaviour patterns are essential, again as is the case in many animal species. A female cheetah may induce copulatory behaviour in the male by crouching down low, and the male will move until he is behind the female. If the female turns to face the male, or moves into any other position such that the male is no longer behind her, this action can have the effect of completely disrupting copulatory behaviour in the male, and in fact, can disrupt the whole courtship. The male may terminate the courtship altogether, or he may start certain of the courtship activities again, either behavioural or vocal. If the female fails to react or moves away, the courtship can be prematurely ended. If the female responds the process may recommence. The breeding animals remain in close contact for two or three days during which copulation is infrequent and usually takes place during early evening or at night.

Rather interesting observations of male behaviour have been made by Ann van Dyk at De Wildt Estates. On a few occasions when a female was crouched down eating, a male approached and tried to mount her. Sometimes the female rose up, threatened the male, and moved off. On one occasion, however, the female just carried on eating and although the male mounted her, actual copulation did not take place. The female in question was in oestrus. The role of an unwilling partner was reversed on another occasion involving two other animals. Ann van Dyk had released a young male into a two hectare enclosure which was occupied by an oestrous female. After the preliminaries had been dealt with, the female, who was obviously ready to receive the male, crouched down low, her tail in a lateral position. The young male approached her, but instead of carrying through the expected sequence, he bit her in the tail. The courtship then terminated.

The third stage of courtship finds the animals quite solicitous and agreeable towards one another. The male is very attentive and follows the female about, and she lies down in front of him and rolls on her back. During this stage, if fertilisation has taken place, the female undergoes hormonal changes in preparation for pregnancy.

That tiny cub you were holding is the result of a highly specialised courtship between adult male and female cheetah. A courtship that contains certain essential basic elements. A courtship that is subtle. If the thread is broken somewhere along the line, either by male or female or by some other external interference the process may be discontinued. A complex courtship.

We obviously do not have all the answers, otherwise there would be more and more cubs born in captivity. But perhaps the solution is indicated in the contents of an interesting letter I received from Mr Bill York who bred cheetah on his ranch in Kenya. During the course of erecting fences on his ranch he happened to enclose several cheetah, five males and two females in one enclosure of eight hectares and in a second enclosure of two hectares there were four males and two females. Within these areas were Thomson's gazelle. Three litters were born in the eight hectare enclosure and two litters in the two hectare enclosure, and all the cubs survived until they were eventually released. In each case Bill York first saw the cubs only when they were about two months old. In similar vein, John Spence only knew about the birth of two cheetah cubs at High Noon Game Farm in the Cape Province when the adult cheetah were being fed. He noticed that one of the females had enlarged mammae which were moist. A hasty search was made and two cubs, a few days old, were found. John Spence feels that to breed cheetah successfully in captivity a number of factors must be present. A high ratio of males to females, a suitable environment and diet, and the cheetah must not be handled at all. This was the case at both the ranch in Kenya and High Noon Game Farm. Leaving the animals to sort themselves out and interfering as little as possible seems to me to be a sensible approach.

Invariably, there are set-backs and disappointments. At De Wildt Estates two females mated during 1974 and later showed a slight lateral swelling. At a calculated gestation of 85 days one of the females displayed signs of labour, going off her food and showing a slight vaginal discharge. The second female showed the same symptoms. The females may have been pregnant, but pseudo-pregnancy is more probable; this is known to have occurred in other species such as the lion, as recorded by Schaller in his work *The Serengeti Lion*. Stimulation of the cervix during copulation may induce a pseudo-pregnancy and at the approximate gestation period the animal may actually go into labour and some bleeding may result.

There have up to now been a number of cheetah cubs born in captivity. The earliest recorded captive birth dates back to the time of Akbar the Great, when one of his cheetah produced a litter of three cubs, all of which survived. In 1950, Dr H. Hediger termed cheetah "non-breeders in zoological gardens" and suggested then that the problem might be psychological or physiological. In more recent breeding programmes at Whipsnade, Montpellier and the Beekse Bergen Park, attention is being given to the siting of cheetah pens to allow a wide range of vision, including a view of the activities of various other animals. In March 1956, at Philadelphia Zoo, a female cheetah gave birth to three cubs, and a year later the same female produced another litter of two cubs, but all five died at an early age. From 1956, about 140 cubs have been born in captivity, representing 44 litters, and the survival rate is about 57%. At first glance these figures may look impressive but there is no reason to believe that we now know why cheetah do or do not breed in captivity. Certainly, some cheetah are breeding, but only about 29 females have actually produced litters. Our knowledge and understanding of this animal has undoubtedly increased over the years, and valuable work has been done and knowledge gained from a number of safari parks and zoos in the United States of America and Europe where cheetah have bred successfully. We are only now beginning to reach the stage where we are gaining some insight into the basic requirements of this animal, which is important to facilitate the continued survival of this species.

There appears to be a certain amount of dispute as to whether cheetah are seasonal breeders or not. Most felids are polyoestrus which indicates that they are not seasonal breeders and are capable of producing offspring at different times of the year. Cheetah, too, are polyoestrus, and furthermore, it appears that breeding times of cheetah vary from one locality to another and even within localities where these animals occur. Eaton believes that cheetah births in East Africa may be seasonal. Eleven of 15 estimates of the times of birth of captive and wild cheetah showed them to have occurred during a period from March to the end of June. The stages of development of cubs were plotted against the rainfall for Masailand, which includes the Nairobi National Park and the Masai Amboseli Game Reserve. The main rains in these areas occur in March and April, when game is widely scattered over the plains and large concentrations of game are rare. From October to February, a second, less intensive and irregular rainfall occurs. The female cheetah goes through three stages when raising her young, and Eaton's comparison of these stages with the rainfall season revealed the pattern shown in Table XI. He believes that the

26 An oestrous female with a male on either side. The one on the right displays the typical expression
of a male cheetah immediately after smelling an oestrous female

27 Oestrous female on the right with two males. These two photographs were taken at the Cheetah
Research Centre at De Wildt Estates where five captive litters were born in April and May 1975

Table XI: *Three stages of growth of cheetah cubs in relation to the seasons in East Africa*

STAGE	AGE OF CUBS	SEASON
1	Birth to six months, female suckling cubs	Peak of rainy season and low concentration of game
2	6-12 months, tuition of cubs	Dry season and high concentration of game
3	12 months and older, cubs can now hunt	Rainy season and low concentration of game

Table XII: *Breeding times*

LOCALITY	BREEDING TIMES	REFERENCE
Southern Africa:		
Transvaal (Kruger National Park)	"during the last half of the year"	Stevenson-Hamilton (1947)
Transvaal (Kruger National Park)	March-April (largest numbers reported); some as early as November	Brynard & Pienaar (1958/59)
Transvaal (Kruger National Park)	usually during fall or winter months	Pienaar (1963)
Transvaal (Kruger National Park)	autumn and winter ("data inconclusive")	Fairall (1968)
Northern Cape Province (Kalahari Gemsbok National Park)	no significant breed-ting season	Labuschagne (pers.-comm.)
South West Africa	December or January	Von Wilhelm (1931/32)
Northern Rhodesia (now Zambia)	March or April	Ansell (1960)
Zambia	November, March, April	Smithers (1966)
East Africa:		
Nairobi National Park	May and late August	Graham & Parker (1965)
Nairobi National Park	early May (1 litter), April-June, Nov.	Eaton (1970)
Masai Amboseli Game Reserve	April to June	Eaton (1970)
Serengeti National Park (Tanzania)	January to August	Schaller (1973)

timing of births relative to the concentration of game is important, because when the cubs are 6 to 12 months old, the female is faced with a trying task. The cubs are growing fast, they need more and more food but are not yet able to hunt for themselves and so contribute nothing towards the food supply. The female has to provide food for herself and her offspring, and at the same time "teach" them how to hunt. During the dry season in East Africa, large concentrations of game are experienced which is advantageous to the cheetah family, as this coincides with the cubs' growing needs. It is Eaton's contention that conditions would favour those females who give birth to cubs in accordance with the timing of seasonal changes.

Seasonal timing of the birth of young does occur in other animal species. Turnbull-Kemp writes that leopard are capable of breeding at any time of the year, "but there is some indication that breeding peaks of common available food animals may happen to coincide with peaks of leopard cub production, which is a common feature in animal behaviour, and this period in tropical countries often tallies with the early rains in areas where rainfall is seasonal". Regarding cheetah births, Turnbull-Kemp indicates that if there *is* any trend in seasonal breeding, cubs seem to be born towards the start of the rainy season. It would seem advantageous if cheetah births were to be synchronised with seasonal changes in the game concentration and the availability of susceptible young prey. But Labuschagne has told me that in the Kalahari he did not detect any breeding season and in fact he saw a number of adult female cheetah each with cubs of *varying* ages. This implies that, in the Kalahari at least, cheetah are capable of reproducing at any time of the year.

In the Serengeti in East Africa, Schaller found that births "were fairly evenly distributed between January and August", and no cubs were known to be born between the months of September and December. Heavy rainfall in the Serengeti occurs from late October or November to December, and the dry season starts in late May, which is preceded by another wet season in the months of April and May. This seems to a degree to contradict the pattern indicated by Eaton, but both samples are small, and indeed Schaller points out that his sample of 14 litters was too small to prove a breeding season. Certainly, seasonal timing of the birth of cubs in some areas is a possibility, but there is a further factor which should be taken into consideration. When a female cheetah loses her entire litter, she will come into oestrus again within a short time, "presumably in response to the sudden cessation of the suckling stimulus". Pippa, the tame but living free female cheetah demonstrated this trend. After losing her first litter when the cubs were about six weeks old, she mated again

Table XIII: *Birth record of Pippa, the tame but living free female cheetah in northern Kenya*

LITTER	CUBS BORN	REMARKS	OESTRUS	BIRTH TO OESTRUS
1st	March 1966 (3 cubs)	cubs killed at 6 weeks of age	female mated in 3 weeks	9 weeks
2nd	August 1966 (1♂:3♀)	litter survived	female mated when cubs mature	16 months
3rd	March 1968 (4 cubs)	cubs killed at 2 weeks of age	female mated in 1 week	3 weeks
4th	July 1968 (3♂:1♀)	Pippa died when her cubs were about 16 months of age		

87

within three weeks. When her third litter was killed, at 13 days, she mated again within a week. Both times she conceived. But after the birth of her second litter, Pippa did not mate until the cubs, which survived, were 16 months old. Birth to oestrus times vary substantially, and a comparison of these times is given in Table XIV.

Oestrus is generally held in abeyance when a female is suckling her young, but when she comes on heat her condition is communicated to males by the presence of sex hormones in the urine. Eaton kept a female with cubs of about 5½ months old under observation until the cubs were about ten months old, and at no time did adult males approach the family group during this period, indicating that the female was never in oestrus. In contrast to this, Pippa apparently came into season every five to seven weeks, and Joy Adamson feels that once the first litter has been born, the female cheetah has the capacity to produce a new litter every 2½ months. At a private zoo near Rome a captive female came into oestrus about 3½ months after the birth of a litter, and thereafter oestrous periods lasting about 15 days occurred regularly with about ten days in between. At Whipsnade Park in England a female came into oestrus 15 days after her second litter had been removed from her (the cubs were about nine months old), and a mating was recorded. That was in April 1969. In June 1969 another mating was observed, and at the end of October 1969 the male was seen to follow the female closely around the enclosure, and although no mating was observed, she produced a litter in the following February. On a previous occasion when a litter was removed from this same

Table XIV: *Birth to oestrus in wild and captive cheetah*

LOCALITY & REFERENCE	BIRTH TO OESTRUS	
Northern Kenya (Adamson 1972)	9 weeks	
Northern Kenya (Adamson 1972)	16 months	same female
Northern Kenya (Adamson 1972)	3 weeks	
Philadelphia Zoo, U.S.A. (Ulmer 1957)	10 months	
Whipsnade Park, England (Manton 1970/1)	7 months	same female
Whipsnade Park, England (Manton 1970/1)	15 months	
Rome (Florio & Spinelli 1967/68)	8 months	
Montpellier Park, France (Vallat, pers.comm.)	15 months	
Montpellier Park, France (Vallat, pers.comm.)	14 months	same female
Montpellier Park, France (Vallat, pers.comm.)	8 months	
Beekse Bergen Safari Park, Holland (Tong, pers.comm.)	19 months	

female (the cubs were about five months old), the female came into oestrus two months later.

The overall impression gained is that cheetah are polyoestrus, their cycles are not geared to the seasonal changes of the areas in which they live. It is apparent that a female, if she loses an entire litter, will mate again quite soon after the loss, and this may happen at any time of the year.

28

29

28 & 29 A mother and her cub.
Note the mantle on the cub

9 Mother-Cub Relationship

The female cheetah, when ready to give birth to her young, adjourns to a pre-selected nursery or lair, situated usually in tall, long grass, or under trees with branches drooping onto the ground, or perhaps in thick underbrush or amongst rocks. After a gestation period of some 90–95 days, the cubs are born, and they come into the world blind, weighing about 300 grams. Little is known about the length of time a cheetah is in labour, or of the actual birth itself, but some information is available from two captive births which occurred in Rome. In the one, only one cub was born, and two hours elapsed from the first contraction to the expulsion of the cub. In the other, three cubs were born. The placenta, expelled soon after the birth, was eaten by the female and she broke the fetal membranes of each cub with her teeth. The umbilical cord, which is "about the thickness of a man's little finger", fell off when the cubs were three to four days old. The cubs weighed from 250 to 300 grams at birth, and one cub measured about 65 cm from the tip of the nose to the root of the tail.

As time goes by, one observes a tiny cub, quite foreign in appearance from its parents except for the characteristic tear line, change from a blind, utterly defenceless creature into a fully grown predator. Some observed growth rates of cheetah cubs are recorded in Table XVI. The opening of the cubs' eyes at about 10 to 12 days (one of the cubs born in a private game park opened its eyes at the exceptionally early age of four days) coincides, more or less, with their first deliberate movement, that of crawling. The colour of their eyes is initially dark gold but clears to a light gold as the cubs grow older. By the age of three weeks the cubs are walking, if somewhat unsteadily, and at six weeks they are able to follow their mother around her hunting terrain.

Many times during the first few weeks of the cubs' life the mother cheetah will move her cubs to new surroundings, carrying one at a time by the scruff of

Table XV: *Gestation periods of captive cheetah*

GESTATION	REFERENCE
92 days	Ulmer (1957)
91-92 days	Florio & Spinelli (1968)
*91 days	Manton (1970)
*95 days	Manton (1970)
*94 days	Manton (1971)
*94 days	Manton (1974)
92-95 days	Herdman (1972)
94 days	Skeldon (1973)

*=different litters

its neck. Schaller relates a delightful episode of a mother cheetah moving her four cubs. After she had moved all of them, one at a time, she twice returned to the previous spot and searched, giving the impression of being "unable to count with precision". No published information makes clear why the mother cheetah so frequently moves her cubs. Joy Adamson records that Pippa moved one of her litters 21 times in the first six weeks, and another litter 14 times in six weeks. Labuschagne also observed females in the Kalahari moving their cubs frequently in the early weeks after their birth. Possibly, several factors determine when and why young cubs are moved.

The lair may become unsuitable due to dampness, or "flea-ridden". Another factor, and quite possibly an important one, could be that the frequent moving is an attempt by the adult female to prevent other large predators from detecting the cubs. And perhaps the odour of a well used nursery would attract the attention of such other large predators, although I have no factual evidence to support this. Even though the adult female may eat the waste products (an activity observed in a captive female), cub smells may still be detectable.

Between the ages of three and six weeks, the deciduous teeth begin to erupt. The upper and lower canines appear first, followed by the upper and lower incisors (but not always in that order, the lower canines or incisors appearing before the top ones in some individuals), and then the upper and lower premolars. The milk teeth of the cubs are very small when compared to

Table XVI: *Growth rate of cheetah cubs at Whipsnade Park, England*

AGE (days)	SEX	WEIGHT (kg)
1st litter:		
139	♀	9,5
	♀	8,6
	♂	10,0
2nd litter:		
65	♀	3,5
	♀	3,8
	♂	3,4
137	♀	10,7
	♀	9,3
	♂	10,6
352	♀	25,0
	♀	28,6
	♂	25,0
3rd litter:		
44	♀	2,30
	♂	2,68
64	♀	3,85
	♂	4,15

At Krefeld Zoo in Germany, two cubs weighed 370 gm each at three days of age. They gained weight steadily at the rate of about 40-50 gm a day. At 5½ months they each weighed 8,5 kg

the milk teeth of lion and leopard cubs, and in form they differ as well. Dr Robert Broom, one of South Africa's most distinguished scientists, wrote of the upper milk canine of a cheetah cub, which has three distinct cusps, "It is quite unlike those of either the lion, leopard or the true cats . . . it is quite a small tooth . . . if such a tooth were found isolated in a fossil deposit, one would be apt to consider it the anterior premolar of a small carnivore". The second upper premolar is also a small tooth and has a "chisel-like" appearance. The third upper premolar is the carnassial (used for shearing flesh). The fourth premolar is so small that it would seem to serve no useful purpose. The lower milk canine also has three distinct cusps and the third lower milk premolar is well developed with four distinct cusps. The fourth lower milk tooth is similar to that of the leopard, except for the posterior cusp, which is better developed. Broom commented on the milk dentition, "It is interesting to note that while the milk teeth, and especially the canines, differ greatly from those of the cats there is a little more resemblance between the cheetah and the lion than between it and the leopard".

The cubs keep their milk teeth until they are about eight months old, at which stage these teeth fall out and their permanent teeth make their appearance. Between the time of the deciduous teeth falling out and the permanent teeth becoming fully established, the cubs may experience difficulty in tearing meat off a carcass, but this stage of their development does not last for long. At nine months the cubs usually have a full complement of permanent teeth, although the age at which this happens, may to some small degree vary with individuals. The milk teeth of lion and leopard cubs start erupting at about three weeks, much the same as with cheetah cubs. However, lion and leopard do not acquire their permanent teeth until they are one year and older, as against about nine months for cheetah cubs.

At about five to six weeks of age, cubs may be introduced to meat for the first time and this coincides, more or less, with the appearance of their milk teeth. The mother allows the young cubs to tug at the carcass of her kill while she is feeding, and they manage to tear off minute pieces of meat. It has been recorded that the cubs will eat meat which has been regurgitated by the female cheetah, a behavioural trait found in the family Canidae. At the age of 18 days a captive cub ate donkey meat which had been regurgitated by the adult female. But this behaviour has not been observed in wild cheetah, although it may possibly occur when the cubs are less than six weeks of age and too young to follow the mother on her hunting expeditions. Because cheetah are inclined to eat too much too quickly they may well vomit up any excess, and if cubs are present it would not be difficult to construe this as a deliberate action.

Young cubs are very playful and mischievous, they tumble about with complete abandon, and it is not an uncommon sight to see the cubs tugging at mother's tail, or nibbling her face. Wide eyed and alert, they are ready to pounce on any imaginary prey, or to scuttle, if somewhat unsteadily, after falling leaves, only to scamper back to mother, who is tolerant towards the antics of her cubs. Play also involves simulations of hunts, one cub being the predator, another the prey. Stalking, taking advantage of shrubs or fallen tree branches, a

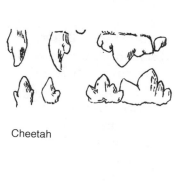

Cheetah

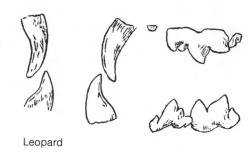

Leopard

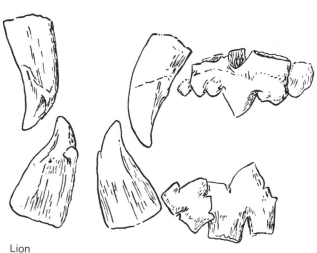

Milk teeth (reproduced from the
Annals of the Transvaal Museum,
by Robert Broom 1949)

Lion

cub at such play will finally pounce triumphantly on its "prey". No serious fighting takes place and the "hunt" usually ends in a general tumble about. This is all part of the learning process of the cubs, and as with most things, practice is needed. Although some of the hunting technique appears to be instinctive, such as stalking, possibly the principles are inherent but the process is learnt. Play time for young cubs is not simply a means of passing the day, it has functional values as well. Obviously, the exercise keeps the cubs in tip top physical condition, but just as important, cubs at play are learning. Watch a young cub dart after a falling leaf. He sniffs it, pats it, paws it. Next time he will pounce on it. Co-ordination and accurate timing are important for a predator. This could spell the difference between life and death when hunting the real thing. When to pounce, when to strike out with a forepaw, this is critical if the cheetah is to have a meal. In this context, it is worthy of note that when cheetah cubs are at play, they often knock each other over with a stroke of a forepaw, an action which will be employed with the utmost precision when they are fully grown.

By three months of age, the cubs are usually weaned. Although the mother's supply of milk is dwindling, one or two cubs will always try now and again to suckle. One captive cub was observed trying to suckle from its mother when it was six months old. It seems that no specific number of mammae has

30 & 31 Family,
mother and
her offspring

been established for cheetah. Available data is meagre and perhaps if many recordings were to be made some sort of conformity in the numbers would become evident. It has been suggested that felids have a normal maximum of four pairs of mammae, and that odd numbers would be abnormal. Pippa apparently demonstrated this abnormality as she had thirteen mammae. Although mammae are usually paired (except in the case of some marsupials) other records also exist of odd numbers of mammae. At De Wildt, two female cheetah were examined while immobilised, and one was found to have six pairs of mammae but the other had five pairs plus a further single mamma on the left side. Individual variations do occur in some species, and in some this may be considerable. But the significance of this variation is not clear.

At ages of less than three months, the cubs, who are extremely playful, quite often become a hindrance to the mother when they accompany her on hunting expeditions. Not yet having become interested in these hunting manoeuvres, they often play about, and in many instances alert potential prey herds. But at three months of age the cubs undergo a sudden change and become intensely aware of their mother's activities, and although they stay hidden in tall grass when she makes her final assault, they eagerly watch her every movement. It was observed in the Serengeti that when a female cheetah was successful in bringing down a prey animal, she would "emit a short cry", announcing her success, and her cubs would be on the scene very quickly. Eaton believes that the cubs are able to find their mother at a kill by the black markings behind her ears, which could act as a "follow me" signal. But it is inevitable that, at times, the female will be hidden from the cubs, and possibly the calling of the mother is a more effective aid than anything visual.

Up to the age of three months, the cub's back is covered by a thick mantle of long bluish-grey or smokey grey hair. This mantle, which is about 7 to 8 cms in length, conceals the tiny spots on the cub, which can only be seen when the mantle is parted, and this often leads to the belief that young cubs are unmarked. Cubs are not born with the mantle, it only appears after birth, but I have been unable to establish from the literature available exactly at what age this occurs. In response to enquiries, people who have bred cheetah in captivity informed me that the mantle was already developed when the cubs first emerged from their nest. Mr V.J.A. Manton, curator at Whipsnade Park indicated that the mantle was already present at 14 days, and John Spence said the mantle was fully developed when the cubs emerged from their nest at the age of 10 to 18 days. Roger Porter, who examined a wild cub aged about 18 days in the Timbavati area in the Transvaal, told me that it did not have a

Table XVII: *Composition of the milk of a female cheetah*

WATER %	FAT %	PROTEIN %	CARBOHYDRATES %	ASH %	REF.
76,8	9,5	9,4	3,5	1,3	Shaul (1962)

mantle, and Willie Labuschagne told me of a cub in the Kalahari aged three weeks which lacked its mantle. Normally, captive cubs are born within a private enclosure and do not venture forth for some two weeks, so it is difficult to say with any certainty exactly when this body hair appears. At about three months of age the mantle begins to fall off and only a scruff of hair remains about the shoulders. The mantle disappears completely when the cubs reach maturity, leaving only the slight mane on the neck. With the progressive loss of the mantle the cubs become less infantile in appearance, and take on a closer resemblance to their parents, albeit in miniature. This mantle serves as excellent camouflage when the cubs are crouched in dry grass or bush cover, enabling them to blend in well with the natural surroundings. On the other hand the mantle and hence the cubs become very conspicuous against green grass which could make the young cubs extremely vulnerable. And, if the purpose of the mantle is camouflage, then why doesn't it last longer than three months? Perhaps the mantle plays a role in *threat* behaviour, assisting in the cubs' *defence,* as the mantle has the effect of making a cub appear larger than it actually is. The female must leave her young when hunting and if a smaller predator, such as a jackal, should find the cubs, the invader would be more easily put off by the threats of a comparatively larger defender.

A mother cheetah, like all mothers, will defend her young if she is able to. Cheetah are easily flushed, and there are a number of records of a mother cheetah being disturbed and running off in fright, giving the impression of not even attempting to defend her cubs. In the Serengeti, Professor Grzimek unwittingly flushed two cheetah cubs, and the mother, who was some 50 metres away, rose furiously and rushed at the car, and continued to run beside it for a while. Whether a female cheetah with cubs will defend her young, George Schaller wrote me, depends entirely on the size of the predator. If a lion comes near the cubs, the female cheetah circles the lion, and threatens by holding her head low, and moaning. She may even attempt short rushes. But Schaller very much doubts that the cheetah would physically attack the larger predator. He wrote that he once saw a female cheetah carrying a young cub attacked by a lioness. The cheetah dropped her cub and did not attempt to defend it, whereupon it was killed by the lioness. In response to hyaena and leopard moving close to a female with cubs at a kill, the cheetah will again employ threats, or she may simply trot off with her young. Schaller has seen a cheetah swat a hyaena, and he believes that a mother cheetah might actually attack the smaller predators if her cubs are in danger. The reluctance of a female cheetah to attack a large predator in defence of her young should not be construed as weakened maternal responsibility. Finding her own life, and thus her potential for producing more litters, endangered, her apparent cowardice may rather be interpreted as an instinctive attempt to protect the reproductive potential of the species.

By the age of seven months the cubs begin taking part in hunts. The female will not kill the prey herself, but instead she will assist the cubs to do so, either by cutting off the escape route of the intended victim, or by bringing to the cubs a live prey animal that she has caught. The adult female doesn't actually *teach* her cubs *how* to hunt. She merely provides them with suitable opportunities, such as releasing a live prey animal to them, and the cubs are thus able to improve their technique each time. Young cubs of this age are not yet able to bring down their own prey successfully, and it is only after many such opportunities which the adult female presents to them, that they gain the necessary expertise. In the Nairobi National Park, a female and her four young were observed stalking a family group of warthogs. When the adult female cheetah was within about 20 metres of them, she suddenly lashed out, causing the group to scatter. The female then placed herself between the adult warthog and her young, while the cubs enthusiastically chased the young piglets. Although the female cheetah could easily have caught one of the warthogs, she refrained from doing so, rather giving her cubs the opportunity to bring down their own prey. In the Serengeti, a female cheetah was observed to carry a young Thomson's gazelle fawn by its head to her waiting cubs. The fawn was still alive, and when she dropped it in front of the cubs it jumped up, the cubs in hot pursuit. The cubs tried to bring the fawn down with a forepaw, but without success, and after some two minutes, the mother cheetah who had been watching the attempts of her cubs intently, killed the fawn. On another occasion, also in the Serengeti, three cubs, aged 15 months, flushed a fawn out of some grass, and after about 18 unsuccessful attempts at knocking it over, the

Growth of cheetah cubs

black cub, 7 days old, lacking mantle. Eyes closed

black cub, 14 days old, showing start of growth of mantle. Eyes open.

mother again came to their aid and bit it in the neck. It was still alive, however, but crouched down, at which point the cubs immediately surrounded it and one of the cubs took it by the throat. On each of these occasions, the adult female watched while her cubs tried again and again to knock over and hold down a young prey animal. She always helped when it became evident that they were too inept at taking it. Through such activities the cubs become more and more adept and gain an ability vital to their future existence.

When the mother has made a kill, she opens the carcass, usually on the flanks, and allows the cubs to feed. The whole family shares amiably and, although minor tussles may take place between the cubs over some small delicacy, no serious fighting breaks out. A companionable atmosphere prevails – "One cub grabbed a meaty bony from its sibling and five minutes later the former casually took it back". After their meal the mother and the cubs lick each other's faces, purring loudly, which says Schaller, is a "utilitarian as well as perhaps a social gesture". An interesting comparison can be made between the social behaviour of lion and cheetah at feeding time. The social system of lions is apparently well developed, yet the system appears to break down when they congregate at a kill. Aggressiveness amongst members of a pride of lions at a kill is not uncommon. Lion cubs tend to be disdainfully treated by adults, and are often injured and sometimes even killed outright when attempting to join

cub, aged 2 months,
showing full mantle

cub, aged 5 – 6 months,
showing ruff on the neck

99

the adults at feeding. Cheetah at a kill behave amicably, and generally aggression is minimal. An injury to a cheetah, however minor, may be critical, far more so than an injury to a lion. After feeding cheetah move away from their kill immediately, and an injured cub would be extremely vulnerable to other predators. An adult cheetah only slightly injured may find itself unable to hunt successfully. A lion on the other hand, even if unable to hunt, is usually sure of a meal since every member of the pride does not take part in every hunt. And lions remain at a kill for longer periods than do cheetah.

At 12 months, cheetah cubs may initiate some of their own hunts even though they are not yet able to hunt successfully without the aid of their mother. Schaller saw cubs aged 15 months, still unable to kill, being helped by their mother. Some two weeks later, Schaller again saw this family, and on the following day, mother and offspring had separated permanently. It was noticed that the cubs lost weight immediately after the break from the mother, but they did survive. Schaller recalls that about four months later he saw one of the female cheetahs from this litter, and watched her as she successfully killed a fawn. Between 13 and 16 months the cubs attain physical and sexual maturity and some of the mane, now much shorter, remains on the neck. Although the cubs are sexually mature at this age, it appears that the females do not conceive until the age of about 21 to 24 months, what one might call deferred maturity. One captive female, a cub from the second litter born at Whipsnade Park, appeared to be coming into season for the first time at the age of nine months, but did not then produce a litter.

The final phase – which is the parting of the family group – has now been reached, and the splitting up of this hitherto close-knit family unit is determined, to a large extent, by the prevailing environmental conditions. In the Nairobi National Park where cheetah density is "high", cubs may stay together and form litter groups, but in the Serengeti where cheetah density is lower, the family group may split up completely, each male and female living a solitary existence. The mother cheetah will, when the group has separated, begin to raise another litter. The break is sudden, and for the cubs the change in circumstances is dramatic. Often the cubs are still unable to hunt well, but they must now fend for themselves. "There is no gradual severing of bonds – it is an abrupt transition from dependence to complete independence", says Schaller. But after the separation the cubs' learning proceeds rapidly and he found no evidence of death from starvation in that age class.

10 *Mortality*

Relatively few reports have been published on numbers and exact causes of cheetah deaths, but we do know that disease and parasites take their toll. However, due to the lack of extensive field work in this direction, one cannot accurately assess the extent to which disease may, or may not, limit cheetah population numbers. Three years ago it was recorded that the death rate among young cheetah in the Kruger National Park was "very high" and at one stage consideration was given to a plan to capture some young cheetah within the Park, and after the administration of any necessary treatment, their subsequent release; but Dr V. de Vos informs me that this project has never in fact been put into operation. There are a number of diseases to which cheetah are susceptible and in most instances where the disease is arrested in its early stages, treatment is successful.

Rickets, a disease of the skeleton which can lead to paralysis, is found to occur in captive more often than in wild cheetah, although rickets has been "frequently" diagnosed in wild cheetah in the Kruger National Park. This disease is generally caused by a lack of calcium during the early formative years in the life of a cub, and the animals suffering from rickets will usually recover if they are given the necessary minerals, calcium and phosphate, and vitamins, particularly C and D. Infectious feline enteritis, commonly known as "cat flu", is a highly contagious disease, which has killed "many" cheetah in the Kruger National Park. This disease can be successfully controlled by preventative immunisation. (Synonyms for infectious feline enteritis are feline distemper, feline infectious panleucopenia, malignant feline panleucopenia and feline agranulocytosis.) Cheetah are also susceptible to rabies, a virus infection from which recovery is rare, and the infected animals die in agony. A number of cheetah have been vaccinated against rabies using the "Onderstepoort rabies vaccine". Cat mange, caused by the external parasite *Notoedres cati* has been diagnosed in cheetah in the Kruger National Park and in some cheetah imported from South West Africa during 1969. External parasites, such as mites, ticks, etc., may be present in animals that are, to all outward appearances, healthy. But these parasites will become active if, as occurs in the translocation from one area to another, the animals are crowded together in paddocks during a quarantine period prior to their release into new surroundings. Some cheetah that developed this mange had been kept in strict isolation for six weeks and more before release into the Kruger Park, and the authorities at the Park set to work quickly once the mange had been diagnosed.

The affected animals were immobilised and then bathed in an anti-parasite dip, which is usually an effective method of treatment. However, caution should be taken when bathing the animals. A few cheetah have died after they were bathed in a malathion solution, and Dr Eddie Young feels that more research

101

on this aspect should be undertaken, especially if this dip is to be used in conjunction with chemical immobilising agents. Dr de Vos recently had to immobilise a cheetah which he encountered near the Lower Sabie camp in the Kruger National Park. The animal was in poor condition and was found to be suffering from *Notoedres cati* and an unidentified ringworm infection, and one of his assistants contracted a bad case of ringworm as a result of handling this animal. This is an example of cheetah fitting into the zoonosis pattern, which is the transmission of disease from animals to man and vice versa. Cheetah infected with this mange lose their body hair and become extremely thin and weak, and in this condition would obviously be susceptible to the hardships and dangers of life in the wild.

Internal parasites can be fatal, particularly to young cheetah. These parasites (round worm, tape worm, flukes, etc.) are generally found in the digestive tract, liver, lungs and sometimes other tissue. Infestation of internal parasites does not usually manifest itself until the animal shows clinical signs such as extreme thinness, dysentery, or a distended abdomen. The administration of suitable worm killing preparations is usually successful. Hepatozoon-like parasites were discovered in an adult female cheetah introduced into the Hluhluwe Game Reserve in Zululand from South West Africa. Two months after its arrival, the animal died. It was in a poor physical condition and was heavily infested with ticks. Extensive wounds around the perineum (the anal region) caused by the ticks carried severe secondary bacterial infection, but it was uncertain if this cheetah died from "hepatozoonosis, or a combination of this, the tick infestation and the secondary bacterial infection", says Dr Mike Keep who, until recently, was stationed at Hluhluwe Game Reserve. Two cheetah cubs from northern Kenya were found to be suffering from a spiruroid worm, *Spirocerca lupi,* which is known to occur in the dog, fox, wolf and cat. One of the cubs died and the other cub eventually responded to treatment. In the Serengeti an adult female, weighing only 23 kg and heavily infested with *Rhipicephalus carnivoralis* ticks, had been killed by lions.

In the Etosha National Park in South West Africa, two cases of anthrax have been diagnosed by Dr Ebedes, until recently the State Veterinarian, although there may have been many more deaths from this disease. Ebedes suspects that rabies may also have been responsible for a few deaths. In many cases the dead cheetah found in the Park were too decomposed for the cause of death to be determined. Ebedes wrote me that cheetah were quite numerous in the Etosha Park during the fifties, but their numbers have declined rather dramatically lately. The cause of this decline has not been established although it is suspected that disease may have played a part. The high mortality rate in the wild is evidenced by the records of the female cheetah which Joy Adamson returned to the wild. This female produced 15 cubs over a period of about 28 months, but only three survived. Other predators accounted for seven cubs (a 47% loss) and disease took the rest.

In captivity, cheetah are prone to a number of diseases which cause a high rate of mortality. It appears that the life span of a cheetah is much reduced once the animal is removed from its natural environment, where it can live for up to

17 years. One may describe even the captive cheetah as an endangered species; van de Werken, who did a survey on captive cheetah gives an *average* lifespan in captivity of 153 cheetah as 3½ years. This survey was completed in the late 1960's, but with increased expertise in the diagnosis and treatment of some of the diseases which strike cheetah it is now possible to lengthen a captive cheetah's lifespan. Van de Werken's survey details the results of post mortems carried out on 123 captive specimens. This reveals that liver diseases killed 33 cheetah (cirrhosis of the liver caused 13 deaths), 31 cheetah died of feline distemper, and tuberculosis accounted for 29. Further mortality factors mentioned are pneumonia and other bronchial diseases, gastritis, enteritis and peritonitis. Nowadays, certain of these diseases can be effectively controlled, for example, immunisation against infectious feline enteritis. Those captive animals which are immunised against this disease are given the *dead* vaccine, which is effective for only one year, and save for one mention of the administration of live feline distemper virus, I have come across nothing to indicate that the *live attenuated* vaccine has ever been systematically used. The live vaccine was at first thought to be a better proposition, but according to the report by Thompson and Vestal which mentions the use of it, this was one of the causes of mortality in the cubs covered by their survey.

Tuberculosis generally strikes cheetah which are kept in confined and damp enclosures, but with the more advanced methods of keeping cheetah in open, natural areas, such as safari parks and sanctuaries, this danger has to a large extent been eliminated. Although immunisation against tuberculosis is available to the human population, I have no record of cheetah being immunised. Dr Oluf Martiny, a member of the National Committee of the South African National Tuberculosis Association (SANTA), mindful of the fact that a number of diseases are transmitted between man and cheetah, suggests that all people who are to handle captive cheetah should be screened first, which is no more than logical. Diet plays a very important role in the wellbeing of captive animals. If they are fed meat which contains too much fat (Bill York has told me that the daily fat intake should not exceed 2%), and the animals don't exercise enough to burn off excess fat, obesity will result. It is not easy to ensure adequate exercise for captive cheetah. A trot or a short gallop once a month is nowhere near enough, they need to run hard and fast every day (or say five days of the week), as they do in the wild state when hunting for their food. Bill York has suggested that the animals run after a light vehicle to which is attached a trailing carcass. He has actually put this method into practice in safari parks in America with the result that the cheetah remained in a healthy and trim condition.

Mortality among captive cubs is high and in many cases the causes of death are unknown. Pneumonia has killed a number of cubs and cases of cannibalism have also been recorded. The males, and sometimes the females, become aggressive and kill the cubs, and in some instances partially devour them. Appendix V lists captive births of cheetah, and where known, the reason for mortality is indicated.

Disease is not the only cause of cheetah fatalities. Strife between cheetah and lion, leopard and hyaena also accounts for a number of deaths. Cheetah, possibly because they are not endowed with powerful jaws, strong teeth and great physical strength, are exceedingly timid in their relationships with other large predators, and also with some non-prey species, such as vultures. They are easily chased off a kill, and as discussed in a previous chapter, cheetah in the Serengeti lost 12% of their kills to lions and hyaenas. In such situations cheetah will display a series of threats towards other animals, but these threats are rarely followed up by any active attack on the oncoming invader, and if the latter pays no heed to the threats the cheetah usually abandons its kill. Very seldom will the threats of the cheetah succeed in keeping the intruder at bay, and if the intruder is not alone, the cheetah practically never succeeds.

Predators are extraordinarily aware of each other, and at times this awareness progresses to a high degree of intolerance. The game of musical chairs is enacted frequently in a predator society, and the predators that usually win are the ones that have size, strength and numbers in their favour. Hans Kruuk relates a number of anecdotes in his outstanding work *The Spotted Hyena,* which provide an insight into the relationships between predators. Two hyaena disturbed a leopard at its kill. The cat took refuge in a nearby tree, and there it was forced to remain while the hyaenas proceeded to tuck into the left over meal of the luckless leopard. On another occasion, Kruuk came across a hyaena eating from a carcass which observations revealed to be a leopard kill; and the leopard still with blood (and no doubt frustration) visible on its face, was secure in the treetops. On yet another occasion, the roles were reversed. A hyaena was at the remains of a gazelle carcass, which he had purloined from a cheetah, and did not notice an approaching leopard. A short scuffle ensued. This time, the leopard emerged the victor and having avenged his species, ran off with the carcass. You might wish yourself to be a lion or a leopard or even a hyaena – but don't think of being a cheetah. They do not have the strength, the size or the numbers to enjoy a peaceful existence in the predator society. Even to the extent of being dispossessed of a kill by vultures, they inevitably come off second best.

This awareness between predators does not only involve the scavenging of another's meal, and the conflicts that occur sometimes result in death. Joy Adamson gives an account of a cheetah cub being killed by a lion, but not eaten, and she says that such occurrences are not infrequent. Lions often chase other predators, including hyaena, leopard and cheetah but not with the inexpressive hunting facial expression, but with bared teeth and vocalisation typical of intra-specific strife. In some cases lions have been known to kill and eat cheetah, and in the Nairobi National Park a lion killed and partially devoured an old male cheetah. In the Kruger National Park two lionesses attacked and severely mauled a pregnant cheetah; another cheetah was seen to abandon a freshly killed impala without eating it because there were lions in the vicinity; and on another occasion visitors to the Park observed two lions seize an impala from a cheetah.

Cheetah and leopard do not normally compete for food although they prey on more or less the same species. The leopard mostly prefers a forest habitat which is not favoured by the cheetah. Nevertheless, interactions between these two predators have been recorded. Leopards eat wild cats up to the size of cheetah, and Mr Ted Davison, first warden of the famous Wankie Game Reserve in Rhodesia and author of the book, *Wankie, The Story of a Great Game Reserve*, told me that he has found fragments of cheetah fur in the stomach contents of a leopard. One day, on discovering signs of a kill in an open vlei, he followed the drag marks which led him to a partially eaten male cheetah. Suspecting a leopard to be the villain, he set a trap over the kill and a medium sized leopard was caught. The stomach contents of this leopard contained cheetah fur. How often leopards kill cheetah is not known, but Ted Davison feels that such occurrences could be fairly frequent. In 1964 in the Kruger National Park, along the Nahpe Road, a large leopard killed a fully grown male cheetah and hoisted the carcass some 3,5 metres onto a branch of a marula tree. The carcass, weighing 45,5 kg, was found untouched, wedged in the fork of this tree. Mike Mills, who is presently studying the brown hyaena in the Kalahari Gemsbok National Park relates a similar incident which took place in the Park in November 1972. He noticed two cheetah lying under a tree and drove closer in order to photograph them. As he approached he could see that the smaller of the two was badly injured about the mouth. The other cheetah moved off, limping badly. About one kilometre further on Mills saw a large leopard. Subsequent events were reconstructed the next day from a study of the spoor left by these animals. The two cheetah, it seems, had moved down to a waterhole after Mills had left and were there attacked by a leopard, presumably the one that Mills had seen the day before. The leopard had killed the younger cheetah, carried it for a distance of some 400 metres and stored it in a tree. The second cheetah had apparently visited the tree, but was chased away by the leopard. Mills inspected the tree two days later and found the dead cheetah still wedged in the tree. The soft parts on the underside and some internal organs had been eaten. One month later the remains of the cheetah were still in the tree, but no more of the carcass had been eaten. Mills concluded that carnivores can determine when an animal is ill or injured, making it vulnerable to attack. It is conceivable though that the leopard may have previously attacked these two cheetah and caused the injuries which Mills noticed. Having been disturbed, the leopard only finished the job when Mills left the scene.

An exceptional type of interaction occurs between cheetah and hyaena, in the form of predation by hyaena on cheetah cubs. It appears that there is a significant relationship between the densities and distribution of hyaena and cheetah in various areas. In the Nairobi National Park where cheetah density is high, the density of other large predators, including hyaena, is low. In fact, hyaena are rare in this Park. In the Ngorongoro Crater, with its excellent hunting terrain and abundance of suitable prey species for cheetah, only an occasional nomadic cheetah is now to be found. The sharp decline of cheetah numbers in this area may be attributed to the apparent increase in numbers of hyaena. Conversely, in the nearby Olduvai Gorge (a bushy habitat), cheetah are more numerous and hyaena few. In the Serengeti and the Masai Amboseli Game Reserves cheetah densities are low, and here hyaena are many.

Labuschagne tells me that in the Kalahari, hyaena predation on cubs contributes to the high mortality rate of cheetah. But this rate of predation appears to be seasonal, and is highest in the summer months. It seems more than coincidental that during these months because of the intense heat, cheetah only hunt from about 5 p.m. onwards, and so young cubs are left alone after sunset. Hyaena are generally nocturnal hunters and while the mother cheetah is away hunting, the hyaena has a clear field. In one particular case Labuschagne reports that an entire litter of cubs was wiped out by a brown hyaena.

Predators that share a common food supply will normally clash. An overlap in the diet of cheetah and hyaena does occur in the Serengeti, but on a relatively small scale as is shown by the predation records. The hyaena is a predator in its own right, but it is also an opportunist and will obtain a meal by the most convenient method possible. A cheetah sprinting after a gazelle on the open plains of the Serengeti is a prominant sight. And a cheetah at a kill on the plains is conspicuous and readily chased off its kills by hyaena. Although the dietary overlap is small, possibly even insignificant, both species take gazelle, gazelle fawns and wildebeest calves. And it is possible that this slight overlap in diet, which occurs for only two or perhaps three months of the year, may prove critical for cheetah. It seems on the surface that hyaena and cheetah have a seasonal interaction in the Serengeti, much the same as in the Kalahari, although for a different reason.

Hyaena are known to dispossess cheetah of their kills, and Schaller found that of the 136 kills he observed in the Serengeti, 4% were taken over by hyaena. Timid though the cheetah is, Schaller does mention one hyaena being slapped in the face when it took a carcass. Typical, though, is the following sequence of events. A female cheetah spots a small fawn among several gazelle. She leaps forward, chases the fawn and catches it. A hyaena approaches, whereupon the cheetah drops the fawn and leaps back as the hyaena takes the carcass and proceeds to eat it, finishing his meal in only ten minutes. A little later the cheetah sees another fawn and catches it, and provides that same hyaena with a second meal. Hardly surprising that in the Serengeti some hyaena follow the cheetah when they migrate with the gazelle herds.

Just to what extent the activities of hyaena limit the population numbers of cheetah is not known. Further research may reveal this. But the interactions between cheetah and hyaena may prove pertinent to the cheetah's survival, especially within game reserves and national parks where both species are to be found.

11 Distribution, Past and Present

Assessing the present distribution of cheetah is not an easy task. Assessing numbers means assessing density, which is the estimated number of cheetah per unit of area within any given territory. Such figures are extremely difficult to calculate because cheetah density is affected by a number of factors, such as the prey species available, the type of habitat, competition from other predators and the expansion of human populations. Moreover, cheetah in some areas are mobile creatures. In the wild they move about considerably, migrating with prey herds and moving out of protected areas and so becoming subjected to pressures from man. One cannot count individual cheetah for no one has devised an accurate method by which cheetah can be counted. Therefore *any* population numbers arrived at are estimates with usually a wide range of possible error. Finally, it borders on the impossible to say that cheetah occur north of some imaginary line but never south of it, so that the locational spread of these animals is not exactly known either.

Distribution of cheetah in the past is equally, if not more, difficult to gauge. There is some literature which deals with distribution in a few areas in the more "recent past", but very little about cheetah is to be found in existing records dealing with the time of the early settlers in South Africa. Quite a number of adventurers cum hunters meticulously diarised all of their day to day encounters. Cornwallis Harris, Andersson, Selous, to name but three, published detailed accounts of their travels into the interior of South Africa. Of encounters with lion and leopard there are many, and descriptions of wildlife in general as recounted by the early explorers show that they were perceptive people. But scarcely a word is mentioned about cheetah. Selous devotes about a page in his book to cheetah and Cornwallis Harris mentions that cheetah were hardly encountered.

If a cheetah is suddenly disturbed it tends to beat a retreat. The animal is easily flushed, for on perceiving approaching danger in the form of man or beast it will often make a move even before the other has become aware of it. In fact I feel that this could be the reason why many hunters found "abandoned" litters; the female cheetah hasn't necessarily abandoned her litter, but has run off in fright. By virtue of the fact that cheetah are so easily flushed, and bearing in mind that cheetah receive scant mention in these early writings, I think it could be assumed that there simply weren't many cheetah around even then. I would feel safe in the deduction that cheetah have never been plentiful.

The great majority of the information which follows, and all the estimated population numbers of cheetah, are drawn from the report by Dr Norman Myers who spent a total of 24 months carrying out a survey commissioned by International Union for Conservation of Nature and Natural Resources (IUCN), on the status of cheetah and leopard south of the Sahara. This was an arduous undertaking entailing visits to some 21 countries in Africa (with a bout of malaria considered no more than an occupational hazard) and massive correspondence with several other countries. Due to the difficulty of evaluating the various factors affecting densities, Norman Myers tells me that the estimate of cheetah numbers may in some cases be termed "intellectual guestimates". Nevertheless, I feel that we now have important information not previously available, which constitutes a guide line to the present status of cheetah in Africa. There have been a lot of cheetah population numbers bandied about lately, usually guess work combined with little or none of the intensive research as was carried out by Norman Myers. A figure of 3 000 cheetah in Africa is often mentioned, but there are approximately that number of cheetah just within protected areas throughout Africa.

AFRICA

Southern Africa

Formerly, cheetah enjoyed a wide range in South Africa, extending from the Cape Province (including the western and midland areas), north to Natal (including the Drakensberg Range), the Orange Free State and the Transvaal. In the Cape Province cheetah were "fairly common" in the Cradock, Uitenhage, Bredasdorp and Swellendam areas, the Albany area (where they became extinct in 1888) and they were also found in the Middelburg and Colesberg areas. Cheetah are now extinct in this province except for small populations which may be found in the northern Cape, and in the Kalahari Gemsbok National Park, where Labuschagne estimates their numbers to be 150. A few cheetah have been introduced onto game farms in the southern Cape Province. In Natal and Zululand, cheetah became extinct in the 1920's. In 1965, 64 cheetah from South West Africa were introduced into the Hluhluwe-Umfolozi Complex in Zululand where they acclimatised quickly and at present their numbers are estimated to be in the region of 110. Recently, I received an unconfirmed report that a female cheetah with young cubs was seen in the Ndumu Game Reserve, but it is not clear if these animals are resident in Ndumu or if they are transients from Mocambique.

In the Transvaal in the days of the early settlers, cheetah, although widespread, did not appear to be very numerous. The early hunters and naturalists in South Africa only rarely mentioned cheetah in the detailed accounts of their travels into the "unknown". But gradually the cheetah's range contracted as the settled and cultivated areas expanded. At present in the Transvaal, cheetah occur in the Kruger National Park, where, Dr Pienaar has informed me, their numbers fluctuate around the 250 mark, and in the wild state there are isolated populations in the north-eastern area. Privately owned game reserves shelter some cheetah though probably not more than 50 or 60 animals. A cheetah sanctuary and an experimental cheetah breeding farm together contain about 30 cheetah.

Cheetah are extinct in the Orange Free State. Mr N.A. Ferreira, mammalogist at the Division of Nature Conservation in the Orange Free State tells me that in 1967, an attempt was made by that body to introduce two cheetah into the Willem Pretorius Game Reserve, but after about a month the animals escaped and one is known to have been shot on a nearby farmland.

Cheetah are classified as "vermin" (at the time of writing) in South Africa, and are not protected should they move outside the game reserves, wherein they enjoy full protection. The cheetah's former range in South Africa has been reduced by 90%, and the estimated number in South Africa is 700 with a range of 600 to 800. By 1980 these numbers could fall to 500 or less.

In the past, cheetah ranged throughout South West Africa, although they probably never occurred along the coastal desert strip. Today, they are less numerous in the southern areas than in the northern parts, where the inland plateaux provide some refuge. The Etosha National Park has some cheetah, but their numbers have been declining since the 1950's, says Dr H. Ebedes. Estimates of cheetah populations in South West Africa vary from 300 to 3 000. But, whether the total be 300 or 3 000, cheetah populations will be seriously reduced unless stringent protective legislation is passed. Cheetah are considered "vermin" and may be shot on sight, and it appears that farm owners are becoming more and more intolerant of this animal.

A quota of 130 live spotted cats are legally allowed out of the country per annum (the declared figure is made up almost entirely of cheetah), but the actual number is probably a lot higher, and Myers estimates that the total annual drain, including supplies for the fur trade, could be as high as 500 cheetah. The situation in South West Africa is crucial since this country and Botswana are about the only two countries where cheetah are found in reasonably large numbers. The estimate for this country is 1 500 cheetah with a range of 1 000 to 3 000. By 1980 the number could be reduced to below 1 000.

Cheetah range in Angola is confined to the drier, arid areas and the Brachystegia biome, and there are no cheetah in the tropical rain forest areas. However, cultivation in the Brachystegia biome and overgrazing by cattle in the arid biome will undoubtedly contribute to the elimination of cheetah habitat, loss of prey species and bush encroachment. Poaching takes place on a large scale, and this factor, together with the pressure on the cheetah habitat, will lead to a sharp decline in the population. Cheetah were declared protected game in 1957, but this legislation is extremely difficult to enforce in a country with only 34 game rangers and where, Myers mentions, the military community is exempt from these provisions of the law. There are a number of protected areas within Angola (the Iôna, Bicuar, Luando, Quicama and Cameia National Parks) which have cheetah. The estimate for Angola is 500 with a range of 200 to 1 000. By 1980 this figure could be half of the present estimate, and then cheetah will be found only in protected areas.

The present range of cheetah in Botswana is wide and extends over about two-thirds of the country. But within this range, cheetah are sparsely distributed. According to Dr Reay Smithers cheetah are not found in the "eastern sector from the Nata River and the northern parts of the Tati

Concession south to near Debeeti". Neither are they found in the eastern parts of Bakwena and Bangwaketse Reserves. I could not establish with any certainty whether cheetah occur in the western sector of Botswana bordering South West Africa and south to the Kalahari Gemsbok National Park. Shortridge does say that cheetah are found in the Gobabis district and "elsewhere in the sand-plain country adjoining Botswana", where he says they increase in numbers quite substantially. But Dr Smithers feels that there is insufficient material to substantiate this claim.

Cheetah have been protected game in Botswana since 1968, but this protection is not altogether effective due to the demand for skins emanating from neighbouring countries where no such legislation exists. Obviously, extensive borders between countries cannot be patrolled but if all countries were to establish an import/export arrangement for skins, a greater check on poaching would be feasible. In the near future, large tracts of land in Botswana are to be declared protected areas, and this may help to reduce poaching. Most of Botswana's export market is made up of livestock and related products, but unscientific farming methods are causing widespread deterioration of the land resulting, in part, in the advancement of bush encroached areas, which are unsuitable for cheetah. The estimate for Botswana is 2 000 with a range of 1 000 to 3 000. By 1980 some reduction is anticipated.

Cheetah formerly enjoyed a fairly wide range in Rhodesia, but today the situation is vastly different. Myers feels that a marked decrease in the numbers of wild predators, including cheetah, will take place within the next ten years. Farmlands are spreading and livestock increasing rapidly, and here too farm owners exhibit increasing intolerance toward any cheetah that appear on their farmlands, whether they are livestock marauders or not. Cheetah are protected animals in Rhodesia, but a marauding animal may be shot. However, the legislation is often abused to the extent that any cheetah sighted is immediately disposed of. Farmers are agitating for the removal of cheetah from the protected list, as many of them are convinced that these animals are on the increase. The frequency with which cheetah are encountered on farmlands may well have increased – due to their wild habitat being taken over by increasingly dense settlements. The overall numbers have gone down, not up. Cheetah populations have already been severely reduced, if not altogether eliminated, in the highveld regions of Rhodesia, and only the Wankie and Gone-Re-Zhou Game Reserves contain modest populations which may total 100. The Matetsi bloc contains about 60 cheetah. Due to development in the lowveld regions, cheetah populations are already declining, and they cannot hope to survive for longer than eight or ten years, if that. The estimate for Rhodesia is 400 cheetah with a range of 250 to 500. By 1980 this figure could probably be reduced to 200, representing cheetah in protected areas only.

Little information exists about cheetah in Mocambique. Poaching is rife and because cheetah numbers are low, they could be eliminated within eight years, possibly less. The estimate for Mocambique is 200 cheetah with a range of 100 to 300. By 1980 cheetah may be extinct in this country.

Malawi is a small country, with cheetah populations now more localised than before. Two parks, the Kasungu and Nyika contain cheetah. Poaching, which was traditional, is now being stopped. The estimate for Malawi is 50 cheetah, with little change expected by 1980.

Although cheetah occur practically throughout Zambia, populations are concentrated in the floodplains and along dambos (dry river beds). Some poaching does occur, but the main threat to cheetah is the expanding human population in the greater proportion of preferred cheetah habitat. Myers feels that most of the cheetah's range in the more suitable habitats will disappear by 1980, so that even if the actual numbers are presently at the maximum of the estimate range it is anticipated that in the near future the populations will be reduced to below 800. In protected areas cheetah are to be found in the Kafue National Park and the Lunga Game Reserve. The estimate for Zambia is 800 with a range of 500 to 2 000. By 1980 the total "will surely fall below 800".

East Africa

A relatively large concentration of cheetah exists in the three East African countries of Tanzania, Kenya and Uganda. The area covered by these three countries contains more cheetah than any other area of comparable size. The total estimate is 3 070 cheetah with a range of 1 600 to 4 750. But various pressures exist and are developing which, within the next five to ten years, could seriously deplete the present cheetah populations.

In Tanzania, poaching is not as rife as in some other areas, although Myers has mentioned that poaching is currently taking the form of shooting from vehicles, and this practice is on the increase. The present ranges of cheetah are the grasslands of Masailand, where some poaching does occur, and a few localised areas of the woodland biomes. The Serengeti/Ngorongoro areas do have cheetah, but land-use trends are creating pressure in these areas. Cheetah are found also in the Ruaha National Park, Mikumi National Park and the Ngorongoro Crater Conservation Area of Tanzania. The estimate for this country is 1 000 or less with a range of 500 to 1 500. By 1980 this figure could fall to as low as 400 cheetah, a 60% drop in a matter of six years.

The former range of cheetah in Kenya was fairly wide although the animals were never abundant. Poaching, which is widespread in spite of the fact that cheetah were given protection in 1955, and trends in the land tenure system are taking a severe toll of the cheetah populations. There are extensive protected areas, but these harbour only small numbers of cheetah. The human population explosion in the south is pushing this species out of previously well established habitats, where ranches and settlements do not tolerate any predator. In the arid land districts of the northern frontier human population pressures are slight and "this is where Kenya's cheetah could best subsist in the future", comments Myers. The estimate for Kenya is 1 900 with a range of 1 000 to 3 000. By 1980, this figure will probably be reduced by 500 to 700.

In protected areas, cheetah are found only in the Kidepo National Park of Uganda and in the wild state small numbers are found in the north-east sector of this country. Little poaching takes place, but in a few years time there will

111

only be small areas left in a relatively undisturbed natural state. The estimate for Uganda is 170 cheetah with a range of 100 to 250. Little change is expected by 1980.

Central Africa

Cheetah have never been present in the rainfall forest region of equatorial central Africa, which includes the countries of Zaire, Congo and Gabon. A few cheetah occur in the south of Zaire, where the development of agriculture is affecting existing cheetah habitat. Congo and Gabon have no cheetah and have not in the past been known to contain any, not any viable populations at least. The estimate for Central Africa is 300 with a range of 100 to 500. By 1980 this figure could be less than 100.

West Africa

A vast tract of land, stretching from the Atlantic Ocean in the west and reaching as far east as the Red Sea, known as the Sahel (the Arabic for "fringe") follows the southern rim of the Sahara Desert. And it is in the West African countries spanning the Sahel that conditions present an extremely serious threat to cheetah. So serious that in the countries of Mauritania, Mali, Upper Volta, Niger, Chad and Cameroon, it is doubtful whether present populations can survive for even ten years. Pressure on cheetah in the form of poaching, more in some of the countries of West Africa than in others, does occur. But the main factor is the reduction of habitat due to man's desiccation of an environment that is already acutely affected by prevailing drought conditions. Another factor which continues to affect cheetah populations is the decline in numbers of prey animals, and unless these are allowed to recover cheetah will be forced away from areas presently occupied, becoming more localised in perhaps not very acceptable habitat. The numbers of cheetah in some of the West African countries, such as Upper Volta, are already extremely low, numbering only 100 cheetah and it is very doubtful if these cheetah will survive the next six years. The cheetah in Niger (200) and Chad (400) could be extinct by 1980. The numbers of cheetah in Senegal, Nigeria and the Central African Republic are also low, and these small populations are unlikely ever to recover at all. There are severe pressures in West Africa, and climatic conditions have aggravated the reduction in the carrying capacity of the land "at the same time that man has begun to overburden an unusually sensitive environment", writes Myers. The estimate for West Africa is 1 700 cheetah with a range of 800 to 2 600. By 1980 this figure could decline to 500 and below.

There are a few protected areas in West Africa, but in total they account for only moderate numbers of cheetah. The protected areas are the Benoué National Park and the Waza National Park in Cameroon and the Saint Floris National Park in the Central African Republic. In Chad, there is the Zakouma National Park and in Ghana the Mole Game Reserve, and extending across the border between Upper Volta, Niger and Dahomey is the W-du-Niger National Park.

North East Africa

The north eastern countries of Sudan, Ethiopia and Somalia, which were also investigated by Norman Myers, have an estimated number of 2 500 cheetah with a range of 1 150 to 4 500. However, by 1980 the numbers could decline to below 1 000. In the Sudan, the present range of cheetah is only in the south, covering some 300 000 square kilometres of savannah woodland. The former range in Somalia, which covered practically the entire country, has been reduced by "half to two-thirds". There are several protected areas in North East Africa, but in the Sudan cheetah are extremely rare if not completely absent in all parks and reserves. Somalia is undergoing extensive agricultural expansion, which has caused a reduction of prey species of cheetah and at the moment, the estimated numbers of cheetah stand at 300. Such small populations are very easily swamped, and the cheetah cannot hope to survive for any length of time. In Ethiopia too, agriculture is spreading rapidly, which means a reduction or complete loss of prey species for cheetah. Poaching in Ethiopia is widespread, a factor which can only speed up the process of extinction. The Sudan banned the trade in cheetah skins in 1972, and as a result poaching there has been reduced.

North Africa and the Middle East

Moving to the north of Africa, we find that up to about 40 years ago cheetah were still found in the mountainous regions of Morocco, bordering the Sahara. Further east, the sandy regions of the Chott el Djerid in Tunisia and the desert south of Tatahouine were once the home of cheetah as well. Today, cheetah are only rarely, if ever, encountered there. The southern regions of Tunisia, which extend into the beginnings of the Sahara, provide some refuge for cheetah where a prey species, the gazelle, is to be found. However, of late, the almost complete extermination of the gazelle has led to a sharp decline in the numbers of cheetah.

Spanish Sahara, Algeria and Libya were most probably also inhabited by cheetah in the past and there may still be some surviving now if their local prey, the gazelle, has not been completely wiped out. Unfortunately, literature on present day status is scanty, if not totally absent, for North Africa. Cheetah existed in Egypt in the distant past and there could still be some there today, but again there is a lack of definite knowledge. I have, however, been informed by an extremely reliable source, that eight cheetah were recently sighted in the Qâttarah Depression in Egypt. The countries north of the Sahara were not investigated by Norman Myers, and so little in the way of up to date literature is available on the position of cheetah there, with the result that it is difficult to give any estimate of cheetah numbers. But if the trend there follows that of other countries, we can justifiably assume that only remnant populations of cheetah survive in Africa north of the Sahara, if there are any left at all.

No reliable information exists of cheetah surviving in the Arabian peninsula since the 1950's. Harrison, in his work, *The mammals of Arabia*, published towards the end of the last decade, writes "It is possible that the species is now extinct in the region". Reports of sightings come through periodically, mainly from the Bedouin, but there is a confusion in the Arabic names for cheetah and leopard. The Arabic for cheetah is *Fahad* or *Fahd,* and this name is sometimes used for the leopard, although the correct name for the leopard is *Nimr.* Further, there have been no specimens of cheetah from this peninsula, except for one collected from Iraq by Dr Norman Corkill in July 1928. These factors make it difficult to gauge the distribution. Prior to the 1950's, however, there were a few reports of cheetah occurring in some of these countries east of the Red Sea. In 1946, two cheetah were sighted in the Sinai Desert, and about 100 years ago cheetah occurred in Israel and Jordan. In 1950, four cheetah were killed in northern Saudi Arabia, just a few kilometres from where the borders of Saudi Arabia, Jordan and Iraq meet, and there are a few other reports of cheetah being killed along oil pipelines in the Syrian Desert. However, the literature does not indicate whether cheetah ever occurred in the central and southern regions of Saudi Arabia. But recently, from Mr John Carter who lived in Oman for over seven years, I heard of a report of a cheetah sighting in December 1968. This occurred some 80 km from the town of Ibri, where a cheetah was seen chasing a gazelle. Mr Carter feels that in all probability this was the last animal in this region and thinks it most likely that the cheetah is now extinct in the Arabian peninsula.

Cheetah may still occur in the more remote parts of Iraq; in the early 1800's they were certainly reported in the low lying areas of the Tigris and Euphrates Rivers, and also in Baghdad, although I think the latter relates to a captive cheetah. Corkill records that in 1925 a cheetah cub was captured at Jumaimah, Muntafiq, in Iraq and two more were taken near Busiya in the Shamiya Desert of southern Iraq where gazelle and hare were numerous. Iran has about 200 and more cheetah at present, due to the magnificent efforts on the part of the conservation authorities in that country. Cheetah occur in Zabol, near the Afghanistan border, and in south-west Iran, where they number about 100.

ASIA

It is interesting to see that cheetah did once range in some Asian countries, although the records are few and far between. Ognev writes that cheetah were found on the eastern shore of the Caspian Sea in the middle of the last century. Afghanistan was reported to have had cheetah in the 1800's, but no recent records exist which indicate whether or not cheetah are still to be found there.

The range of cheetah in the USSR is mentioned by G.A. Novikov as being limited to Turkmenia, where they occasionally occur in the deserts of the southern parts of the Republic, near Atrek, Tedzhen, Murgab and Kushka. Small numbers of cheetah were long ago reported in the north-western and south-western areas of Turkestan, taking in the western slopes of the Tien-Shan, Syr-Darya and the Kyzyl-Kum sandy regions. Small numbers were recorded in the low lying areas of the Syr-Darya as well as the Amu-Darya areas. The diet

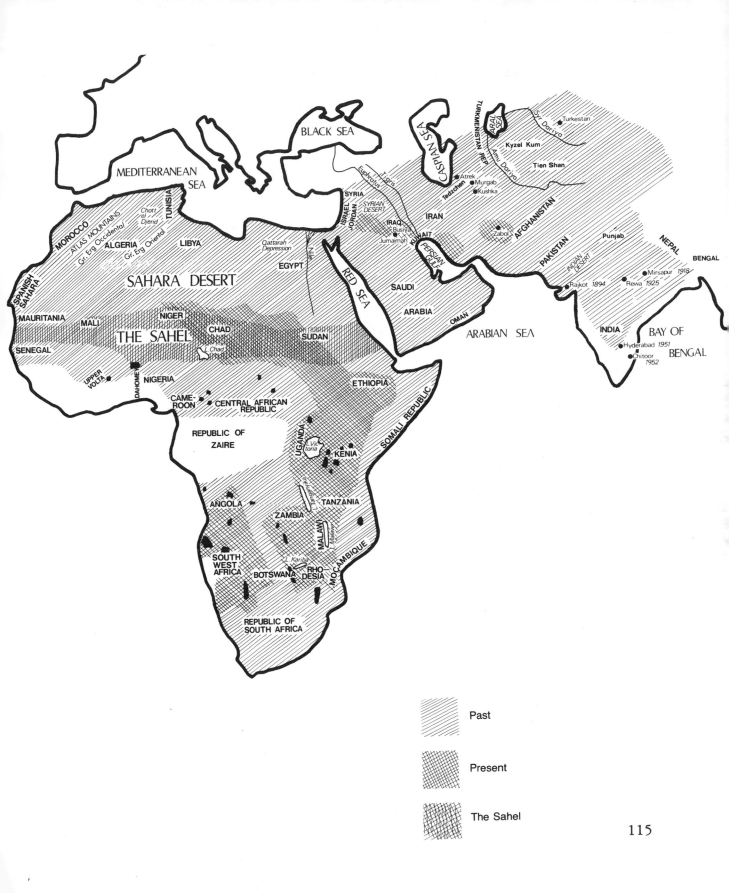

MEDITERRANEAN SEA

BLACK SEA

CASPIAN SEA

TURKMENISTAN REP.

ARAL SEA

Syr Daria

Turkestan

Kyzel Kum

Tien Shan

Amu Daria

Atrek
Murgab
Tedzhen
Kushka

MOROCCO
ATLAS MOUNTAINS
Gr. Erg Occidental
Chott el Djerid
TUNISIA
ALGERIA
Gr. Erg Oriental

LIBYA

SYRIA
SYRIAN DESERT
ISRAEL
JORDAN

Euphrates

Tigris

IRAN

AFGHANISTAN

Zabol

Punjab

NEPAL

Qattarah Depression

IRAQ
Busiya
Jumaimah

KUWAIT
PERSIAN GULF

PAKISTAN

INDIAN DESERT

Mirsapur 1918

BENGAL

SPANISH SAHARA

SAHARA DESERT

EGYPT

Nile

RED SEA

SAUDI ARABIA

Rajkot 1894

Rewa 1925

MAURITANIA

MALI

NIGER

CHAD

SUDAN

OMAN

ARABIAN SEA

INDIA

Hyderabad 1951

BAY OF BENGAL

SENEGAL

THE SAHEL

L. Chad

Chitoor 1952

UPPER VOLTA

NIGERIA

DAHOMEY

CAME-ROON

CENTRAL AFRICAN REPUBLIC

ETHIOPIA

SOMALI REPUBLIC

REPUBLIC OF ZAIRE

UGANDA

Vic-toria

KENIA

ANGOLA

Tanganyika

TANZANIA

ZAMBIA

MALAWI

L. Malawi

MOÇAMBIQUE

SOUTH WEST AFRICA

L. Kariba

BOTSWANA

RHO-DESIA

REPUBLIC OF SOUTH AFRICA

Past

Present

The Sahel

115

List of Game Reserves and National Parks
where cheetah are still living:

1. Umfolozi Game Reserve, South Africa
2. Hluhluwe Game Reserve, South Africa
3. Mkuzi Game Reserve, South Africa
4. Ndumu Game Reserve, South Africa
5. Kruger National Park, South Africa
6. Kalahari Gemsbok National Park, South Africa
7. Gorongoza National Park, Mocambique
8. Wankie National Park, Rhodesia
9. Etosha National Park, South West Africa
10. Iôna National Park, Angola
11. Bicuar National Park, Angola
12. Cameia National Park, Angola
13. Luando National Park, Angola
14. Quicama National Park, Angola
15. Kafue National Park, Zambia
16. Lunga Game Reserve, Zambia
17. Mikumi National Park, Tanzania
18. Ruaha National Park, Tanzania
19. Amboseli Game Reserve, Tanzania
20. Ngorongoro Crater Conservation Area, Tanzania
21. Serengeti National Park, Tanzania
22. Nairobi National Park, Kenya
23. Masai Mara Game Reserve, Kenya
24. Meru National Park, Kenya
25. Kidepo National Park, Uganda
26. Benoué National Park, Cameroon
27. Waza National Park, Cameroon
28. Saint Floris National Park, Central African Republic
29. Zakouma National Park, Chad
30. Mole Game Reserve, Ghana
31. Boubandijidah National Park, Cameroon
32. W-du-Niger National Park, Niger, Dahomey
    and Upper Volta (these are three parks of the
    same name which adjoin the three countries)

of the cheetah in these areas consists of various desert birds, larks, small mammals, such as the Tibetan and other hares. All of these reports date back some considerable time, and I wonder if any cheetah are still living there today. If prey animals have not been exterminated and the cheetah has been left relatively undisturbed, there is reason for the belief that some populations may still survive.

INDIA

Cheetah formerly ranged from the Punjab to Bengal (they did not occur in Nepal) and to the Deccan in the south of India. The last published record of the occurrence of cheetah in India is from Kirkpatrick who saw a cheetah in the Chitoor District in 1952. Mukherjee, zoologist at the Indian Museum in Calcutta, listed records of sightings of cheetah for the last 100 years, the latest of which are indicated on the distribution map. It is generally felt that cheetah are now extinct in India, although from a reliable source, I have received information that a few cheetah were recently sighted somewhere in the Indian Desert bordering Pakistan. But this can in no way be construed as evidence of a stable population.

In the past the range of cheetah covered practically the whole of the African continent, with the possible exception of the equatorial rain belt in central Africa. This range has been drastically reduced and in many of its former areas cheetah are now extinct. In fact, Myers comments that the cheetah population in Africa has probably reduced by half since 1960. In another five or six years we can expect that more of the presently populated areas will be devoid of cheetah, and right now the chances of this trend being reversed or even halted seem to be zero.

12 The Cheetah Crisis

Despite man's age old association with cheetah, and in spite of the additions in more recent years to the literature on this animal, little uniformity emerges concerning the ecology and population dynamics of cheetah. On aspects such as behavioural characteristics, social structure, reproduction and mortality, various opinions have been expressed, based usually on short term and localised field observations. This state of affairs is alarming, in view of the ever dwindling number of cheetah. It becomes more alarming when one realises that of the cheetah living in Africa now, there will only be about half that number left by 1985. And those surviving animals will most probably be found only in game reserves and National Parks. There will be no cheetah living in the wild, or at most, only remnant populations will be left to face ever increasing hazards, such as the disappearance of prey animals and the increasing use, and misuse, of the land. "Grassland savannahs comprise only 5% of Africa and are thus at a premium for both human expansion and the cheetah's survival", writes Dr Norman Myers. Those words sum up the crisis that faces this animal. What chance does the cheetah have when human settlements are reaching out, at an ever increasing pace, grasping and hungrily devouring the remnants of cheetah habitation?

All species, including man, are potentially subject to natural extinction in the evolutionary process. Some have considered the cheetah to be genetically "worn out" by virtue of its long evolutionary history. Even if this were the case, the supreme predator, *Homo sapiens,* has no cause to hasten the process of extinction. Why? Because each time a mammal, a bird, a plant or a fish is forced out of existence, the existence of man and beast on planet earth is jeopardised. The average person living in South Africa is unlikely to feel any real sense of loss when a rare plant becomes extinct in Australia. It is difficult for an Australian to feel any sense of loss when a mammal becomes extinct in the United States of America. The addition of a mammal or a bird to the categories of rare or endangered species passes for the most part entirely unnoticed. But it does in fact concern us all, for there is a link, sometimes tenuous, but there *is* a link between the survival of one species and that of another. I look at it in this way. Picture, for a moment, a turntable on which a disc is poised and delicately balanced. The seas, marshes, rivers, continents, islands, mountains, plants and grasses, forests, and the many different creatures, including man, together keep that balance. Then one species becomes extinct, and a slight tremor starts. But it is rectified, nature has her ways. As time goes on, more and more creatures vanish, plants and trees and forests disappear, and the tremor starts again, increasing in severity as one organism after another is rooted out by man. No longer can nature rectify this imbalance and the tremor gathers force. Because each species has its own niche on earth the elimination of any one can set up a chain reaction which we may not be able to control.

The link between cheetah survival and an imbalance in nature must be more clearly stated. I shall never forget the words spoken to me by Norman Myers when I met him in 1972. It was a chance meeting, but for me a momentous one, one that entirely changed the nature of my interest in cheetah. This meeting really brought home to me the crisis which faces the cheetah. Norman is a modest man, but extremely perceptive and packed full of knowledge and energy, as his book *The Long African Day* indicates. Thinking aloud he said to me: "Could it be that cheetah are an ecological indicator by virtue of the fact that they are so sensitive to the deterioration of habitat?" I reflected on this for a moment or two, at first not comprehending his meaning. But then consider the following. The world demand for beef has spiralled in recent years (more people means more food). Botswana's economy is primarily sustained by the export of beef. In fact three quarters of this country's export revenue is derived from beef. Naturally, under the circumstances, more and more cattle are being farmed to meet the demand. Unfortunately, due to the lack of agricultural and pastoral expertise, the land suffers, and the number of cattle which can be supported by existing grazing areas diminishes. New grazing areas must continually be established, and these suffer in exactly the same manner. Land-use practices have transformed large areas of grassland (where cheetah once lived) into scrub (which is totally unsuitable for cheetah). The survival chances of cheetah in those areas of Botswana into which the livestock industry is now expanding will certainly be adversely affected, Dr von Richter, wildlife ecologist with the National Parks in Botswana, mentioned in a letter he wrote me some time ago. The cheetah's range has shrunk through being taken over by livestock. Areas once inhabited by cheetah in Botswana are now desolate epitaphs of man's unthinking depredation. Botswana is not the only country where mismanagement practices threaten the fertility of the land, for this trend is discernable in a number of other countries. The sacrifice of grasslands and forests to large scale agricultural development represents a further threat to the wild creatures that live in those habitats. In the highlands of Kenya, the local inhabitants are systematically eliminating three forests, hacking down the trees to establish agricultural settlement areas. These forests, the North Nandi, the Kakamega and the South Nandi forests, are unique in that the creatures living there are found nowhere else in the world. And as the over-exploitation of his environment continues, so man places his own survival in jeopardy.

An ecological indicator? Yes, I believe so. The steady decline in the cheetah populations in almost every country in Africa should indicate that there is something amiss. But man is undaunted, the signs are not heeded.

During the last few years of intensive development of farming and ranching in Rhodesia, direct conflict between man and predator has become more pronounced. Marauding animals are not a recent phenomenon but the extreme antagonism in the methods of eradication of these predators is something new. It is unreservedly acknowledged that the farmer must protect his interests, but when one lamb is taken on a farm and shortly thereafter a farmer announces that he has shot six cheetah because they have killed his livestock, then I begin

32

33

32 & 33 Mischievous
and alert

to feel uneasy. In Rhodesia, although cheetah are protected, farmers may shoot marauding animals, but there is now agitation for the complete removal of cheetah from the protected list, due it is said, to the increased numbers encountered on farms. Similarly, in South West Africa, a dealer in live cheetah is convinced that cheetah are on the increase because they are sighted on farmlands more frequently than in the past. But surely this is more logically accounted for by the fact that areas hitherto spared from agricultural development are being taken over by ranches and farms and there is just nowhere else for the cheetah to go, except perhaps to migrate from the new farms to the older farms.

A consequence of the rapid agricultural development is the decrease, and in some areas complete extermination, of prey animals suitable to the cheetah. In addition, poaching of wild herbivores has further depleted the cheetah's natural food supply. This problem can be overcome if we are prepared to tackle it. Iran has shown that it can be done. From about 15 years ago livestock numbers have been regulated and legislation prohibiting poaching has been enforced, all of which contributed to the recovery of wild prey populations. The results of this approach are encouraging, for there has been a marked increase in the numbers of cheetah.

While on the subject of man versus cheetah on farmlands and ranches, it is as well to discuss another hazard which the cheetah faces; the capture of live cheetah for the export market. In South West Africa, three organisations undertake the capture and export of live cheetah to zoos and safari parks. Traps are usually set up at certain trees which males regularly mark, and one organisation uses the faeces of female cheetah as bait in the traps. With this method of capturing cheetah, more males than females are captured and one count revealed that nine out of ten animals captured were males. Another organisation found that about three quarters of the captured animals were males. Over and above the population reduction caused by the capture of cheetah, the imbalance of the sexes caught could pose a further threat to the wild population. It is generally considered that more than one male is necessary for successful courtship, so the question to be asked is: "How does this affect the reproduction of wild cheetah?" The South West African authorities allow a quota of 130 spotted cats to be exported from that territory per annum. However, Norman Myers has recorded an annual drain on the cheetah population, for live export as well as the fur trade, of 500 cheetah. The official 130 is made up almost entirely of cheetah, because leopard breed successfully in zoos and there is thus an available source of supply. The same cannot be said of cheetah. Nevertheless, the demand for cheetah is increasing, mainly from Europe and North America, and one South West African organisation involved in this trade has stated that the world market could absorb at least 500 cheetah a year from South West Africa. Scientific captive breeding, if this can be achieved, may alleviate the problem of the high demand from zoos and safari parks aggravating the dwindling supply from wild populations.

International communication between various breeding farms, safari parks and zoos would be of tremendous value to the scientific management of breeding programmes. Since 1970 the number of captive cubs born has increased over previous years, but very often the reasons why cheetah are able to produce a litter at one place while not at another, are unknown. Some knowledge of the components of a successful programme has been contributed by various people, and it would seem that a large area, set in natural surroundings, strict dietary control and rigorous exercise are some of the basics. A pooling of knowledge and results of research may open the way to the successful breeding of cheetah in captivity. The supply of captive bred cheetah to zoos and other similar organisations would be a feasible proposition, but the re-stocking of game reserves requires more and careful thought. As we have seen, a cub growing up in the wild has the opportunity to *learn* to fend for itself before it *must* fend for itself. How would a captive bred cheetah fare if suddenly confronted with a wild environment?

There is a further complication. Cheetah densities vary from area to area, in some reserves cheetah numbers are said to be "high" and in others they are "low". But, do we really know how many cheetah there should be in any particular area? Could not the introduction of more cheetah to a "sparsely" populated area place too heavy a burden on that particular habitat? To elaborate a little further. In the Serengeti, densities have been calculated to be one cheetah to every 100 to 125 sq km. Cheetah in the Nairobi National Park have been roughly estimated at one to every three to six sq km. In the Amboseli, the average density is about one to 32 sq km. In South Africa, the Timbavati Private Nature Reserve (which is approximately 600 sq km) has an estimated number of 30 cheetah, and Labuschagne has calculated a figure of 150 cheetah in the 9 600 sq km of the Kalahari Gemsbok National Park. And the Sahelian zone, along the southern Sahara fringe, has densities of self-maintaining populations reaching as low as one cheetah to every 320 sq km. One tends to assume that in all areas, except the Nairobi National Park, cheetah densities are "low". But perhaps these "low" densities are not really low at all, but just right for cheetah. If a cheetah population in any given protected area fluctuates about a certain figure or if the population remains "low" in spite of excellent hunting terrain and an abundance of available prey species, can we not assume that the population has reached equilibrium with its environment? Where then is the justification of introducing more cheetah without first having established what is "low" or "high", "scarce" or "numerous"? The results could be catastrophic. If we create an artificially high density for cheetah in an area where they have previously been sparse, the stress of the situation could cause an outbreak of disease, endangering the entire resident population. I become concerned when I hear of ideas to immobilise, translocate and release cheetah from wild populations into game reserves. As Myers points out, cheetah do not lend themselves to the usual form of the "sanctuary strategy" method of protection. A comparison is drawn with the Bengal tiger. Already endangered, the Bengal tiger can be adequately protected in game reserves and parks. Within a 500 sq km area (about the size of Johannesburg), at least five and sometimes ten times as many tiger can be protected as can be achieved for cheetah in a similar sized piece of savannah.

Thus their density requirements make it difficult indeed to introduce simple conservation programmes. The first essential is that we gain the necessary knowledge to introduce workable programmes; at present far too much effort is being expended by far too many people in unco-ordinated and diverse conservation manoeuvres. While a great deal of effort is being expended in directions detrimental to the cheetah's chances of survival. Long term studies, co-ordination of effort and a ubiquitous desire to live in a world of real live nature are needed before we shall make any real progress.

All this could be achieved. If people cared enough. Right now that disc on the turntable is shuddering.

APPENDIXES I–V

Appendix I: *Classification of cheetah*

Kingdom: Animalia
  Phylum: Chordata
    Sub-phylum: Vertebrata
      Class: Mammalia
        Sub-class: Theria
          Infra-class: Eutheria
            Cohort: Ferungulata
              Super-order: Ferae
                Order: Carnivora
                  Super-family: Feloidea
                    Family: Felidae
                      Sub-family: Felinae[1]
                        Genus: *Acinonyx*
                          Species: *jubatus*

Generic synonymy following Allen (1939):

Acinonyx Brookes, Cat. Anat. and Zool. Mus. of Joshua Brookes, p. 16, 1828. Type species
    Acinonyx venator Brookes = *Felis venatica* H. Smith.
Cynailurus Wagler, Natürl. Syst. Amphib., p. 30, 1830. Type species *Felis jubata* Linnaeus.
Guepardus Duvernoy, L'Institut, Paris, 2:145, 5 May 1834. Type species not specified; includes
    Guepardus flavus Schreber (pl.105) and *Felis guttata* Hermann.
Guepar Boitard, le Jardin des Plantes, p. 174, 1842. No type specified; included *Guepar jubatus*
    (Schreber) and *Felis guttata* Hermann.
Cynofelis Lesson, Nouv. Table Règne Anim., Mamm., p. 48, 1842. Included *Felis jubatus* Schreber
    and *F. guttata* Hermann, of which the latter is excluded, leaving the former as type species.
Gueparda Gray, List. Spec. Mamm. Brit. Mus., p. 46, 13 May, 1843. Type species *Felis jubata*
    Schreber.
Note: Ellerman, Morrison-Scott & Hayman (1953) delete *Guepardus* and *Cynofelis* from the
    synonymy, saying "The former is based on *Felis guttatus* Hermann, which is unidentifiable but
    certainly not a cheetah, and the latter is a substitute for the former".

Acinonyx jubatus jubatus (Schreber, 1777).
Felis jubata Schreber, Säugthiere, 3:392, 586, pl. 105, 1776, Cape of Good Hope. Erxleben,
    1777. Thunberg, 1811a. A. Smith, 1826. Smuts, 1832. A. Smith, 1834.
Felis fearonii A. Smith, South African Quart. Journ., 2:245, 1834, Northeast of Natal.
Felis fearonis Fitzinger, Sitzb. K. Akad. Wiss., Wien, math.-nat. Cl., 59:sect. 1, pg. 664, 1869,
    Cape of Good Hope.
Felis lanea P.L. Sclater, Proc. Zool. Soc. London, p. 532, Oct., 1877, Beaufort West, Cape of
    Good Hope. Layard, 1878. P. L. Sclater, 1884.
Acinonyx guttatus obergi Hilzheimer, Sitzb. Ges. Naturf. Freunde, Berlin, p. 289, text-f.2, 1913,
    Ketmannshoop,[2] South West Africa.

---

(1) Harrison (1968) and Dorst and Dandelot (1970) use the sub-family name of Acinonychinae

(2) Correct spelling is Keetmanshoop

Acinonyx rex Pocock, Abstr. Proc. Zool. Soc. London, no. 283, p. 18, 1 Mar. 1927; Proc. Zool. Soc. London, p. 250, pl. 1 (col.), text-f. 6, 8, 6 Apr. 1927, Umvukwe Range, northwest of Salisbury, Rhodesia.[3]
Distribution: Angola, Zambia, southern Congo (K.), southern Tanzania, Mocambique, Malawi, Rhodesia, Botswana, South West Africa, South Africa.

Acinonyx jubatus raineyi Heller, Smithsonian Misc. Coll., 61: No. 19, pg. 9, 8 Nov. 1913. Ulu Station, Kapiti Plains, Kenya Colony.
Acinonyx jubatus velox Heller, Smithsonian Misc. Coll., 61: No. 19, pg. 7, 8 Nov. 1913. Agate's, Loita Plains, Kenya Colony.
Acinonyx guttatus ngorongorensis Hilzheimer, Sitzb. Ges. Naturf. Freunde, Berlin, p. 290, text-f.3, 1913. Ngorongoro, south of Lake Natron, Tanganyika Territory.
Distribution: Kenya, Uganda and Tanzania.
Note: *A. guttatus ngorongorensis* was described from a zoo specimen and is considered "doubtfully valid" even although differing in colour and pattern (Smithers 1968).

Acinonyx jubatus soemmeringii (Fitzinger, 1855).
Cynailurus soemmeringii Fitzinger, Sitzb. K. Akad. Wiss. Wien. math.-nat. Cl., 17: pt. 2, p. 245, 1855. Steppes of Kababish, south of Bajuda Desert, Kordofan, Anglo-Egyptian Sudan.
Felis megabalica Heuglin, Leopoldina, Amtliche Organ K. Leop.-Carol. Deutsch. Akad. d. Naturf., 4: No. 3, p. 23, May 1863. West bank of Bahr-el-Abiad, Anglo-Egyptian Sudan.
Acinonyx wagneri Hilzheimer, Sitzb. Ges. Naturf. Freunde, Berlin, p. 285, 1913. Kordofan.
Distribution: Ethiopia, Chad, northern Cameroun, northern Central African Republic, northern Nigeria, southern Niger.
Note: "The zone of transition between this eastern sub-species and *hecki* of Senegal does not appear to have been investigated". (Smithers 1968).

Acinonyx jubatus hecki Hilzheimer, 1913.
Acinonyx hecki Hilzheimer, Sitzb., Ges. Naturf. Freunde, Berlin, p. 288, text-f. 1, 1913. Senegal, West Africa.
Felis jubata senegalensis Blainville, Ostéographie, Felis, atlas, pl. 10, 1843. Senegal.
Distribution: southern Mauritania, Senegal, east to Haute Volta, southern Mali and northern Dahomey.
Note: The name *senegalensis* was used by von Meyer (1826) for *Felis leo senegalensis*. Blainville's *senegalensis* is thus a homonym and invalid. (Meester, pers. comm.).

Acinonyx jubatus venaticus (Griffith, 1821).
Felis venatica Griffith, Vert. Anim. Carnivora, p. 93, 1821. India.
Acinonyx venator Brookes, Cat. Anat. and Zool. Mus. Joshua Brookes, 16, 33, 1828. India.
Acinonyx raddei Hilzheimer, S.B. Ges. Nat. Fr. Berlin, 291, 1913(?). Merv. Transcaspia.
Distribution: North Africa from Morocco to Egypt, southern Asia and India.

(3) Should be Macheke (see chapter on the king cheetah)

Approximate geographical areas within which sub-species of the cheetah occur.

Appendix II: *Table of weights and measurements*

LOCALITY	SPECIES/SUB-SPECIES	SEX	MASS (kg)	TOTAL LENGTH (metres)	HEAD & BODY (metres)	T... (m...
East Africa:						
Kenya	—	F	63	2,36	—	—
Kenya	—	M	62	2,24	—	—
Kenya	—	M	58	2,01	—	—
Kenya	—	M	65	2,13	—	—
Kenya	—	M	59	2,11	—	—
Kenya	—	F	—	1,91	—	—
Loita Plains, Kenya	*A.j. velox*	M	—	—	1,30	0,
Loita Plains, Kenya	*A.j. velox*	F	—	—	—	—
Kapiti Plains, Kenya	*A.j. raineyi*	M	—	—	1,24	0,
?	*A.j. velox* and *raineyi*	M (Min)	—	—	1,12	0,
		(Max)	—	—	1,13	0,
?	*A.j. velox* and *raineyi*	F (Min)	—	—	1,14	0,
		(Max)	—	—	1,25	0,
South Africa:						
Kruger Nat. Park	—	M	59	2,01	—	—
Kruger Nat. Park	—	M	50	2,02	—	—
Kruger Nat. Park	—	M	49	2,01	—	—
Kruger Nat. Park	—	F	58	—	—	—
Eastern Transvaal	—	—	—	2,03-2,31	—	0,
Kruger Nat. Park	—	M (av)	54	2,06	—	0,
Kruger Nat. Park	—	F (av)	43	1,90	—	0,
Transvaal	*A.j. jubatus*	M (Min)	—	—	—	—
		(Max)	—	—	—	—
Albany Dist.	*A.j. jubatus*	F	—	—	—	—
Umfolozi River	*A.j. jubatus*	F	—	—	—	—
Botswana:						
Mababe	—	M	—	1,88	—	0,
Gomoti River	—	F	39	1,86	—	0,
Rhodesia:						
Macheke Dist.	*A. rex*	M	—	—	—	—
S.W. Rhodesia	*A. rex*	M	—	—	—	—
?	*A. rex*	—	—	—	1,27	0,
?	*A. rex*	—	—	—	1,35	0,
?	*A. rex*	—	—	2,06	—	—
?	*A. rex*	—	—	2,21	—	—
N.W. Rhodesia	—	—	—	2,22	—	—
N.W. Rhodesia	—	—	—	2,20	—	—
Korea ESA	—	M	—	1,96	—	—
Korea ESA	—	M	—	1,94	—	—
Korea ESA	—	M	—	1,93	—	—

OULDER HEIGHT (tres)	SKULL:TOTAL LENGTH (mm)	REFERENCE
34	—	Meinertzhagen (1938)
6	—	Meinertzhagen (1938)
4	—	Meinertzhagen (1938)
31	—	Meinertzhagen (1938)
9	—	Meinertzhagen (1938)
	—	Shortridge (1934)
	200	Roosevelt & Heller (1914)
	171-178	Roosevelt & Heller (1914)
	191	Roosevelt & Heller (1914)
	192	Roberts (1951)
	193	Roberts (1951)
	162	Roberts (1951)
	173	Roberts (1951)
86	—	Roberts (1951)
	—	Roberts (1951)
	—	Roberts (1951)
	—	Roberts (1951)
	—	Shortridge (1934)
88	—	Labuschagne (PC)
85	—	Labuschagne (PC)
	192	Roberts (1951)
	193	Roberts (1951)
	168	Roberts (1951)
	172	Roberts (1951)
	—	Smithers (1971)
	—	Smithers (1971)
	203	Roberts (1951)
	203	Roberts (1951)
	—	Pocock (1927)
	—	Pocock (1927)
	—	Cooper (1927)
	—	Cooper (1927)
	—	Shortridge (1934)
	—	Shortridge (1934)
	—	Van Ingen & Van Ingen (1948)
	—	Van Ingen & Van Ingen (1948)
	—	Van Ingen & Van Ingen (1948)

Appendix III: *Ecto- and endoparasites of cheetah*

(A) Ectoparasites (those found externally);
(B) Endoparasites (those found internally);
(C) Protozoal parasites (those occurring in the blood)

PARASITE		*REGION				REFERENCE
SCIENTIFIC NAME	VERNACULAR NAME	K	Z	E	EA	
(A)						
Haemaphysalis leachi leachi	Dog tick		X			Baker & Keep (1970)
Hyalomma truncatum	Bont legged tick		X			Baker & Keep (1970)
Amblyomma hebraeum	Bont tick		X			Baker & Keep (1970)
Rhipicephalus appendiculatus	Brown ear tick		X			Baker & Keep (1970)
R. maculatus	—		X			Baker & Keep (1970)
R. simus	—		X			Baker & Keep (1970)
R. carnivoralis	—				X	Schaller (1972)
Notoedres cati	Mange mite	X				Young (1972)
(B)						
Taenia acinonyxi	Tape worm			X		Ebedes (pers.comm.)
T. leonina	Tape worm			X		Ebedes (pers.comm.)
Ancylostoma sp.	Tape worm			X		Ebedes (pers.comm.)
Spirocerca lupi	—				X	Murray *et al.* (1964)
(C)						
Eperythrozoon felis	—				X	Murray *et al.* (1964)
Babesia canis	Biliary				X	Adamson (1969)

K = Kruger National Park; Z = Zululand; E = Etosha National Park; EA = East Africa
*region from which parasite recorded

Appendix IV: *Chemical immobilisation*

Recommended doses of Sernylan and Ketamine (dosage rates in mg/kg)

*†SERNYLAN	†KETAMINE	REFERENCE
0,4-0,8		Ebedes (1970; 1973)
0,8		Seal *et al.* (1970)
	6,3	Smuts *et al.* (1973)

*A dosage rate of 0,8 mg/kg body weight should NOT be exceeded as this may cause severe convulsions leading to death (Ebedes 1973)
†There is no specific antidote to these drugs (Harthoorn 1973)

Medication that may be administered to control some side effects (Ebedes 1973; Young *et al.* 1972; Harthoorn 1973; de Vos, pers. comm.)

SIDE EFFECT	CONTROL	RECOMMENDED DOSAGE mg/kg
Muscle spasms and convulsions	Acepromazine maleate	0,05 to 0,10
Muscle spasms and convulsions	Triflupromazine hydrochloride	0,1
Muscle spasms and convulsions	Azaperone	0,4 to 0,6
Muscle spasms and convulsions	Xylazine hydrochloride	0,5 to 0,7
Salivation, only if excessive	Atropine sulphate	0,5 to 1
Hypoventilation	Doxapram hydrochloride	0,5 to 1 (this may be repeated at 5 min. intervals to a total dose of 2)

Dosage rates and reaction times using (a) KETAMINE (Smuts *et al.* 1973; Meltzer pers. comm.) and (b) SERNYLAN (Ebedes 1970; Pienaar *et al.* 1969; Smuts *et al.* 1973)

	SEX	APPROX. AGE (years)	APPROX. MASS (kg)	DOSAGE (mg/kg)	TOTAL AMOUNT (in mg)	TRANQUILLISER (in mg)	ATAXIA SETS (in mins.)
(a)	♂	5-6	47,30	10,6	500	—	2
	♂	5-6	47,30	6,3	300	—	5
	♀	3½	45,00	6,7	300	—	5
	♀	4-5	60,00	7,5	450	—	7
(b)	♂	—	36,40	1,1	40	—	—
	♂	3-4	38,60	0,7	30	+10 Siquil	—
	♂	4-5	40,90	0,9	40	+12 Siquil	—
	♀	—	47,30	1,3	60	+20 Azaperone	—
	♂	—	—	—	60	+20 Azaperone	—

*Death due to anoxia caused by vomited food particles plugging the glottis (de Vos, pers.comm.)

Chemical and trade names of drugs mentioned
(from *The capture and care of wild animals* 1973)

ACTIVE INGREDIENT	TRADE NAME	MANUFACTURER
Acepromazine maleate	Acetylpromazine	Boots Pure Drug Co.
Atropine sulphate		
Azaperone	Stresnil	Janssen Pharm.
Doxapram hydrochloride	Dopram	A.H. Robins & Co.
Ketamine hydrochloride	Ketalar, Ketanest, Vetalar	Parke-Davis & Co.
Phencyclidine hydrochloride	Sernyl, Sernylan	Parke-Davis & Co.
Triflupromazine hydrochloride	Siquil	Squibb Labs.
Xylazine hydrochloride	Rompun	Bayer

Notes on post-capture treatment:
1. Hypostasis (fluid on the lung) may be avoided by turning the animal over once an hour.
2. As a measure for the prevention of the possibility of shock, undue noise and activity in the immediate vicinity of the animal should be limited.
3. Under field conditions where there is strong sunlight it is advisable to cover the eyes of the animal with a black blindfold to prevent damage to the retina. To lubricate the cornea and prevent drying an ointment should be instilled – ordinary castor oil is excellent for this.

CUMBENT (mins.)	FULL RECOVERY (hours)	REMARKS
	5	—
	2	—
	2½	suffered an epileptiform convulsion 29 mins. after dosage
	—	—
	14	Administered orally
	14	Administered in the hip
	7	Administered in the hip
	1 hr. 15 min.	Little evidence of convulsions
	—	Died in 3 hrs.*

Appendix V: *List of captive births of cheetah (Period 1956 to 1974)*

LOCALITY	BIRTH DATE	NUMBER AND SEX RATIO ♂:♀	REMARKS
U.S.A.			
Philadelphia Zoo	March 1956	2:1	mother became aggressive and killed 1 the other 2 died in 3 days
Philadelphia Zoo	April 1957	1:1	cubs died at 3 months of distemper
Oklahoma City Zoo	April 1962	2:1	1 male stillborn, the female lived 24 h the other male lived 10 days. Litter premature, autopsy revealed kidneys n fully developed
Oklahoma City Zoo	November 1962	1:1?	1 eaten by adult male, other cub lived hours. Litter premature, autopsy revea kidneys not fully developed
Toledo Zoo	December 1971	1:3	all survived
San Diego Wild Animal Park	November 1970	1:2?	2 cubs killed by parents, the male hand-reared
San Diego Wild Animal Park	April 1972	0:3	all survived
San Diego Wild Animal Park	November 1973	0:8	3 died
San Diego Wild Animal Park	November 1973	0:3	all survived
Lion Country Safari, Georgia	May 1973	2:1	1 cub died at 5 weeks, 1 at 14 weeks, survived
Lion Country Safari, Georgia	November 1973	4:1	1 cub died at 3 weeks
Lion Country Safari, Texas	March 1974	1:3	all survived
Lion Country Safari, Texas	May 1974	0:4	all survived
Lion Country Safari, California	January 1973	?1:0	delivered by caesarian section but died
Lion Country Safari, Texas	August 1974	1:1	all survived
Hogle Zoological Gardens, Salt Lake City	November 1973	1:0	cub died
Lion Country Safari, Stockbridge	May 1973	2:1	2 cubs died
Lion Country Safari, Stockbridge	November 1973	4:1	2 cubs died
World Wildlife Safari	September 1973	0:4	?
GERMANY			
Krefeld Zoo	April 1960	4?	1 cub eaten by parents, 1 cub killed by female at 2 days, remaining 2 hand-rea and lived 4 years
?(W. Scheffel)	February 1969	1:1	all survived
ITALY			
Private Zoo, Rome	January 1966	1:0	survived
Private Zoo, Rome	December 1966	3:0	all survived
ENGLAND			
Whipsnade Park	September 1967	1:2	2 cubs survived, 1 female developed osteodystrophic lesions of limbs and di from apparent epileptiform convulsion months
Whipsnade Park	July 1968	1:2	all survived (*one of the litter females prod a litter in Oct. 1972*)
Whipsnade Park	February 1970	1:1	all survived
Whipsnade Park	March 1971	0:3	all survived
Whipsnade Park	October 1972	1:0	survived
Whipsnade Park*	October 1973	2:3	all survived
Whipsnade Park	May 1974	1:0	died after 1 month
Whipsnade Park	September 1974	3?	?
The Lions of Longleat Safari Park	November 1971	1:1	cubs died

136

*The first F2 litter to be born in the world

FERENCE

ner (1957); van de Werken
68)
ner (1957); van de Werken (1968)
np (pers.comm.)

np (pers.comm.)

ldon (1973)
rdman (1972)

rdman (1972); York (pers.comm.)
ompson & Vestal (1974)
ompson & Vestal (1974)
inn (pers.comm.); York
rs.comm.)
inn (pers.Comm.); York (pers.comm.)
inn (pers.comm.); York (pers.comm.)
inn (pers.comm.); York (pers.comm.)
rk (pers.comm.)
inn (pers.comm.)
ompson & Vestal (1974)

ompson & Vestal (1974)
ompson & Vestal (1974)
on (1974); Thompson & Vestal (1974)

cke (1960); van de Werken (1968)

ompson & Vestal (1974)

rio & Spinelli (1967); van de Werken (1968)
rio & Spinelli (1967); van de Werken (1968)

nton (1970)

nton (1970)

nton (1971)
wlins (1972)
nton (1974)
nton (pers.comm.)
nton (pers.comm.)
nton (pers.comm.)
ompson & Vestal (1974)

FRANCE

Montpellier Park	December 1968	2:1	2 males survived, the female died at 1̶ of bronchial pneumonia
Montpellier Park	June 1970	3:1	all survived
Montpellier Park	November 1971	2:2	3 cubs died in 48 hours, the survivor ▮ for 5 months and cause of death undetermined
Montpellier Park	October 1972	2:2	1 male died soon after birth, the other▮ died from infectious bronchial pneumo▮ 4 months, the 2 females survived

CZECHOSLOVAKIA

Prague Zoo	April 1972	2:1	all survived
Prague Zoo	May 1973	3:2	only 1 cub survived

HOLLAND

Arnhem Zoo	1963	2?	cubs eaten by parents within 2 days
Beekse Bergen Safari Park	October 1972	4:1	all survived
Beekse Bergen Safari Park	April 1974	1:4	male born dead, had a mouth malform▮ all the females survived

SOUTH AFRICA

High Noon Game Farm	June 1973	2:0	all survived
Ski-haven Game Farm	October 1974	2?	?
Collisheen Estate, Umhlali, Natal	December 1974	2:3	2 females died at 3 months

Summary:

Total number of male cubs born	59
Total number of female cubs born	66
Unsexed	15
Total number of cubs born	140
Total number of litters born	44
Number of breeding females	29
Survival rate of cubs (survived at least 4 months)	57%

During 1975 at De Wildt Estates, near Pretoria, the following births have taken place:

April 1975	2:1	cubs abandoned by mother, now being hand-reared
April 1975	?2:1	one partially eaten by the mother; one female died at one week due to damage to aorta; one▮ male being hand-reared
April 1975	?1:3	cubs abandoned by mother and three subsequently died; one female being hand-reared
May 1975	4?	being reared by the mother
May 1975	2:3	one cub stillborn; three died from exposure; one female being hand-reared

(1971)

(pers.comm.)
(pers.comm.)

: (pers.comm.)

ipson & Vestal (1974)
ipson & Vestal (1974)

e Werken (1968)
(1974 and pers.comm.)
(pers.comm.)

:e (pers.comm.)
Star" Johannesburg 1974
naar (pers.comm.)

Numbers of litters born in captivity during period 1956-1974.

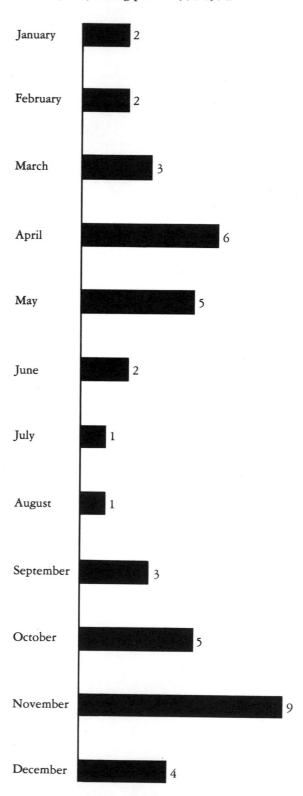

January	2
February	2
March	3
April	6
May	5
June	2
July	1
August	1
September	3
October	5
November	9
December	4

Key to Bibliography

p. 25:   general speed *Meinertzhagen 1955.*
p. 25:   speed given by motorists *Hardy 1959.*
p. 25:   speed in Serengeti *Kruuk and Turner 1967.*
p. 25:   dash at 104-112 km/hr *Howel 1944.*
p. 26:   catches wild rabbits *Grzimek 1963.*
p. 26:   third period of suspension *Hildebrand 1959.*
p. 27:   rotary sequence *Hildebrand 1959.*
p. 28:   extended phase *Hildebrand 1960.*
p. 28:   extra 10 km an hour *Hildebrand 1961.*
p. 28:   cheetah and leopard muscles *Ewer 1973.*
p. 28:   scapula pivots 26° *Hildebrand 1961.*
p. 28:   durations of phases *Hildebrand 1961.*
p. 28-31:   length of stride *Ewer 1973.*
p. 31:   loss of speed in changing lead *Hildebrand 1959.*
p. 31:   frequent change in lead *Hildebrand 1959, Hildebrand 1961.*
p. 31:   stop in one stride *Hildebrand 1961.*
p. 31:   tail not an aid in turning *Hildebrand 1961.*
p. 31:   tail other opinions *Eaton 1970, Labuschagne (PC).*
p. 32:   pads of foot *Ewer 1973.*
p. 32:   walking and trotting *Hildebrand 1961.*
p. 32:   efficient and fast *Hildebrand 1959.*
p. 32:   body posture *Hildebrand 1961.*

5 *Hunting*

p. 34:   both forepaws *McLaughlin in Ewer 1973.*
p. 34:   no evolutionary upstart *Ewer 1973.*
p. 34:   cognisance of wind *Hardy 1959.*
p. 34:   hunting times *Schaller 1968.*
p. 34:   travel *Schaller 1972.*
p. 34:   stalking *Schaller 1968*, no concealment *Schaller 1968.*
p. 34-35:   behaviour of fascination *Walther 1969.*
p. 35:   flight behaviour of gazelle *Walther 1969, Kruuk & Turner 1967.*
p. 36:   stalk minor role *Kruuk & Turner 1967.*
p. 37:   cubs at play *Kruuk & Turner 1967.*
p. 37:   stalking drops out with experience *Eaton 1970.*
p. 38:   open pursuit *Eaton 1970.*
p. 38:   kongoni *Eaton 1970.*
p. 39-41:   no group co-operation *Myers 1974.*
p. 41:   cheetah and black-backed jackal *Eaton 1969.*
p. 41:   cheetah ignore jackal *McLaughlin 1970.*
p. 42:   suffocation *Kruuk & Turner 1967.*
p. 42:   throat bite *Ewer 1973.*
p. 42:   teeth enter braincase *Ewer 1973.*
p. 42:   neck vertebrae dislocated *Leyheusen in Ewer 1973.*
p. 43-44:   dew claw *Burton 1950, Eaton 1972, Ewer 1973.*
p. 44-45:   drag carcass *Schaller 1968.*
p. 45:   distance carcass dragged *Schaller 1968.*
p. 45-46:   breathing rates *Eaton 1969, Schaller 1972.*
p. 47:   doesn't always drag carcass *Stevenson-Hamilton 1947.*
p. 48:   cheetah lose kills *Schaller 1968.*
p. 49:   fails to follow dodging gazelle, slips *Schaller 1968.*
p. 50:   abandons any pursuit *Ewer 1973*
p. 50:   movements of cheetah *Schaller 1972.*
p. 50:   Kafue National Park *Mitchell et al. 1965.*

6 Predation

7 Social Structure

p. 70:   sample of 244 cheetah *Schaller 1972.*
p. 70:   of 1794 in East Africa *Graham 1966.*
p. 70:   cheetah in Botswana *Smithers 1971.*
p. 70:   groups in the Serengeti *Schaller 1972.*
p. 70:   female goes off on her own *Schaller 1972.*
p. 70:   four groups Nairobi National Park *Eaton 1970.*
p. 70:   group leadership *Eaton 1969.*
p. 70:   no mixed groups *McLaughlin 1970.*
p. 70-72:   females with cubs never associate *Schaller 1972, Labuschagne (PC).*
p. 72:   visual encounters *Eaton 1970.*
p. 72:   results of an East African study *Graham 1966;* Kruger National Park mainly in groups *Pienaar 1969;* family groups not uncommon *Hardy 1959.*
p. 72:   relationship of additional adults *Graham 1966.*
p. 72:   male following oestrous female *Eaton 1968.*
p. 72:   females with large cubs *Schaller 1972.*
p. 72:   sex ratio of vertebrates *Skinner (PC).*
p. 72:   male zebra *Skinner (PC).*
p. 73:   adult sex ratios Serengeti *Schaller 1972.*
p. 73:   adult sex ratios East Africa *Graham 1966.*
p. 73:   adult sex ratios Kruger National Park *Pienaar 1969.*
p. 73:   471 live cheetah sexed *Pienaar (PC).*
p. 73:   grid system of recording *Pienaar (PC).*
p. 73:   sex ratio five and fourteen litters *Schaller 1972.*
p. 73:   sex ratio cubs Nairobi National Park *McLaughlin 1970.*
p. 74:   average litter size leopard and lion *Schaller 1972.*
p. 74:   built-in safety mechanism *Myers 1975.*
p. 74:   lion litter sizes Kruger National Park *Pienaar 1969.*
p. 76:   territoriality a fundamental characteristic *Burt 1943.*
p. 76:   home range *Burt 1943.*
p. 76:   not territorial *Schaller 1972.*
p. 76:   time-plan *Eaton 1968.*
p. 76:   ranges overlapped extensively *McLaughlin 1970.*
p. 77:   three possible categories *Labuschagne (PC).*
p. 77:   direct aggression *Stevenson-Hamilton 1947.*
p. 77:   reported cases of cannibalism *Stevenson-Hamilton 1947.*

8 The Process of Reproduction

p. 78:   *lordosis Skinner (PC).*
p. 78:   cycle 7-14 days *Herdman 1972.*
p. 79:   cycle 15 days *Florio & Spinelli 1967.*
p. 79:   response chart adapted from *Herdman 1972.*
p. 81:   sexual anxiety *Herdman 1972.*
p. 81:   mound building *Herdman 1972.*
p. 81:   increase in frequency *Herdman 1972.*
p. 81:   more than one male *Florio & Spinelli 1967, 1968.*
p. 81:   some form of aggressiveness *Manton 1970.*
p. 81:   two males rear up *Schaller 1972.*
p. 81-82:   male interaction to females *Herdman 1972.*
p. 82:   vaginal smears *Herdman 1972.*
p. 82:   dominant male *Herdman 1972.*
p. 82:   male management *Herdman 1972.*

10 *Mortality*

11 *Distribution, Past and Present*

p. 114:   Syrian Desert *Harrison 1968.*
p. 114:   Iraq *Corkill 1929.*
p. 114:   Iran *Myers 1975, McLaughlin 1970.*
p. 114:   Caspian Sea and Afghanistan *Ognev 1935.*
p. 114:   USSR *Novikov 1956.*
p. 114:   Turkestan *Ognev 1935.*
p. 117:   India *Kirkpatrick 1952.*
p. 117:   range reduced *Myers 1975.*

12 *The Cheetah Crisis*

p. 118:   grassland savannahs 5% of Africa *Myers 1975.*
p. 119:   Botswana beef export *Myers 1975.*
p. 119:   eliminating three forests *The Star, Johannesburg, Oct. 15, 1974.*
p. 121:   livestock regulated Iran *Myers 1975.*
p. 121:   more males than females captured *Myers 1975.*
p. 121:   quota 130 spotted cats *Myers 1975.*
p. 121:   annual drain 500 cheetah *Myers 1975.*
p. 121:   world market absorb 500 a year *Myers 1975.*
p. 122:   density Serengeti *Schaller 1972.*
p. 122:   density Nairobi National Park *McLaughlin 1970, Eaton 1974.*
p. 122:   density Amboseli *Myers 1975.*
p. 122:   estimated number Timbavati *Myers 1975.*
p. 122:   estimated number Kalahari *Labuschagne (PC).*
p. 122:   densities in the Sahelian zone *Myers 1975.*
p. 122:   sanctuary strategy *Myers 1975.*

Bibliography

ADAMSON, J. 1969: The spotted sphinx. Collins, London.

ADAMSON, J. 1972: Pippa's challenge. Collins, London.

ALI, S. A. 1927: The Moghul Emperors of India as naturalists and sportsmen. J. Bombay Nat. Hist. Soc. XXXI (4): 833-61.

ALLEN, G. M. 1939: Checklist of African mammals. Bulletin: Museum of Comparative Zoology 83: 232-234.

ANON., 1974: The cheetah and our National Parks. Custos 3 (5): 10-12.

ANON., 1973: Cheetahs for the Kruger Park. Custos 2 (4): 34-37.

ANSELL, W. F. H. 1960: Breeding of some larger mammals in Northern Rhodesia. Proc. Zool. Soc. London 134: 251-274.

ANSELL, W. F. H. 1965: Standardisation of field data on mammals. Zoologica Africana 1 (1): 97-113.

ASTLEY MABERLY, C. T. 1967: The game animals of Southern Africa. Thomas Nelson & Sons, Johannesburg, S.A.

BAKER, M. K. & M. E. KEEP 1970: Checklist of the ticks found on the larger game animals in the Natal Game Reserves. The Lammergeyer 12: 41-47.

BATEMAN, J. A. 1961: The mammals occurring in the Bredasdorp and Swellendam Districts, C.P., since European settlement. Koedoe 4: 78-100.

BAUDY, R. E. 1971: Notes on breeding felids at the Rare Feline Breeding Center. Int. Zoo Yearbook 11: 121-123.

BECKER, PETER 1971: Peoples of Southern Africa – their customs and beliefs. The Star, Johannesburg.

BLANCOU, L. 1960: Destruction and protection of the fauna of French Equatorial and of French West Africa. Part III: Carnivores and some others. Afr. Wildl. 14 (3): 241-245.

BOURLIÈRE, F. 1963: Specific feeding habits of African carnivores. Afr. Wildl. 17 (1): 21-27.

BOURLIÈRE, F. 1964: The natural history of mammals. Knopf, New York.

BOURQUIN, O., J. VINCENT & P. M. HITCHINS 1971: The vertebrates of the Hluhluwe Game Reserve-Corridor (State-land)-Umfolozi Game Reserve Complex. The Lammergeyer 14: 5-58.

BRAIN, C. K. 1970: New finds at the Swartkrans Australopithecine Site. Nature 225 (5238): 1-7 (Reprint).

BRIDGES, W. 1955: The cheetah, the mildest cat. Animal Kingdom 5: 130-134.

BROOM, R. 1949: Notes on the milk dentition of the lion, leopard and cheetah. Annals of Tvl. Museum XXI, Part II: 183-185.

BRYNARD, A. M. & U. DE V. PIENAAR 1960: Annual report of the biologist 1958/1959. Koedoe 3: 1-205.

BURT, W. H. 1943: Territoriality and home-range concepts as applied to mammals. J. Mammalogy 24: 346-352.

BURTON, R. W. 1950: The "dewclaws" of the hunting leopard or cheetah (A. jubatus Schreber). J. Bombay Nat. Hist. Soc. 49 (3): 541-543.

BURTON, R. W. 1959: The voice of the cheetah or hunting leopard. J. Bombay Nat. Hist. Soc. 56 (2): 317-318.

CADE, R. 1965: Cheetah just tolerate humans. Africana 2 (4): 33-35.

CAMPBELL, A. & G. CHILD 1971: International co-ordination and control of ownership and movements of wildlife and its products. Proc. Symposium SARCCUS. September: 85-90.

149

CARVALHO, CORY T. DE 1968: Comparative growth rates of hand-reared big cats. Int. Zoo Yearbook 8: 56-59.

CHAPUIS, M. 1961: Evolution and protection of the wild life of Morocco. Afr. Wildl. 15 (2): 107-112.

CHINERY, M. 1972: Animal communities. Collins, London.

COOKE, H. 1963: Pleistocene mammal faunas of Africa with particular reference to southern Africa. *In* African ecology and human evolution, ed. F. Howell and F. Bourlière, 65-116. Aldine, Chicago.

COOPER, A. L. 1927: Notes on *Acinonyx rex* (Cooper's cheetah). South African Journal of Science XXIV: 343-345.

COOPER, A., M. ELLIS, C. A. W. GUGGISBERG & R. LANWORN 1968: Animals of the world. The Hamlyn Group, London.

CORKILL, N. L. 1929: On the occurrence of the cheetah *(Acinonyx jubatus)* in Iraq. J. Bombay Nat. Hist. Soc. 33 (3): 700-702.

CORNWALLIS HARRIS, W. 1840: Portraits of game and wild animals of Southern Africa. A.A. Balkema, Cape Town (1969).

CULLEN, A. & S. DOWNEY 1960: Saving the game. Jarrolds, London.

DE GRAAF, G. 1974: A familiar pattern deviation of the cheetah *(Acinonyx jubatus)*. Custos 3 (2): 2.

DENIS, A. 1964: Cats of the world. Constable, London.

DE SOUZA, C. W. L. 1963: Groups of animals. Afr. Wildl. 17 (3): 259.

DESROCHES-NOBLECOURT, C. 1963: Tutankhamen – life and death of a pharaoh. George Rainbird, London.

DE VOS, V. & M. C. LAMBRECHTS 1971: Emerging aspects of wildlife diseases in Southern Africa. Proc. Symposium SARCCUS, September: 97-109.

DE VOS, V. 1973: Common infectious and parasitic diseases of captured wild animals. *In* The capture and care of wild animals, ed. E. Young. Human & Rousseau, Cape Town & Pretoria.

DE VOS, V. 1974: Diseases of wild animals. Custos 3 (3): 10-13.

DORST, J. & P. DANDELOT 1970: A field guide to the larger mammals of Africa. Collins, London.

EATON, R. L. 1969: Co-operative hunting by cheetahs and jackals and a theory of domestication of the dog. J. Mammalia 33 (1): 87-92.

EATON, R. L. 1969: Notes on breathing rates in wild cheetahs. J. Mammalia 33 (3): 543-544.

EATON, R. L. 1969: The cheetah. Africana 3 (10): 19-23.

EATON, R. L. 1969: Hunting relationships of cheetahs with non-prey species. J. Mammalia 33 (3): 543.

EATON, R. L. 1969: The social life of the cheetah. Animals 12 (4): 172-175.

EATON, R. L. 1969: The cheetah's survival endangered by man. Def. Wildl. News 44 (1): 57-60.

EATON, R. L. 1970: Group interactions, spacing and territoriality in cheetahs. Z. Tierpsychol. 27 (4): 481-91.

EATON, R. L. 1970: Hunting behaviour of the cheetah. J. Wildl. Management 34 (1): 56-67.

EATON, R. L. 1970: Notes on the reproductive biology of the cheetah. Int. Zoo Yearbook 10: 86-89.

EATON, R. L. 1970: The predatory sequence, with emphasis on killing behaviour and its ontogeny, in the cheetah *(Acinonyx jubatus* Schreber). Z. Tierpsychol. 37 (4): 492-504.

EATON, R. L. 1971: The cheetah – fastest of the world's land animals is racing towards extinction. Afr. Wildl. 25 (4): 123-128.

EATON, R. L. 1972: An experimental study of predatory and feeding behaviour in the cheetah *(Acinonyx jubatus)*. Z. Tierpsychol. 31 (3): 270-280.

EATON, R. L. 1973: Cheetah speed explained. Afr. Wildl. 27 (1): 43.

EATON, R. L. 1974: The cheetah – the biology, ecology and behaviour of an endangered species. Van Nostrand, New York.

EATON, R. L., W. YORK & W. DREDGE 1970: The Lion Country Safari and its role in conservation, education and research. Int. Zoo Yearbook 10: 171-172.

EATON, R. L. & W. YORK 1970: Breeding cheetahs on a large scale. Lion Country Safari, California, U.S.A. Unpublished.

EBEDES, H. 1970: The use of Sernylan as an immobilising agent and anaesthetic for wild carnivorous mammals in South West Africa. Madoqua 2: 19-25.

EBEDES, H. 1973: The drug immobilisation of carnivorous animals. In The capture and care of wild animals, ed. E. Young. Human & Rousseau, Cape Town & Pretoria.

ELLERMAN, J. R. & T. C. S. MORRISON-SCOTT 1953: Checklist of Palearctic and Indian Mammals – Amendments. J. Mammalogy 34 (4): 516-519.

ELLERMAN, J. R., T.C.S. MORRISON-SCOTT & R.W. HAYMAN 1953: Southern African Mammals 1758-1951: A reclassification. British Museum (Natural History) London.

ELOFF, F. C. 1973: Lion predation in the Kalahari Gemsbok National Park. J. Sth. Afr. Wildl. Mgmt. Ass. 3 (2): 59-63.

ENCKE, W. 1960: Birth and rearing of cheetahs at Krefeld Zoo. Int. Zoo Yearbook 1: 85-86.

ERRINGTON, PAUL L. 1956: Factors limiting higher vertebrate populations. Science 124: 304-307.

ESTES, R. D. 1967: The comparative behaviour of Grant's and Thomson's gazelles. J. Mammalogy 48 (2): 189-209.

EWER, R. F. 1973: The carnivores. Weidenfeld & Nicolson, London.

FAIRALL, N. 1968: The reproductive seasons of some mammals in the Kruger National Park. Zoologica Africana 3 (2): 189-210.

FITZSIMONS, F. W. 1919: The natural history of South Africa. Vol. I. Longmans, Green & Co. London.

FLORIO, P. L. & L. SPINELLI 1967: Successful breeding of a cheetah in a private zoo. Int. Zoo Yearbook 7: 150-152.

FLORIO, P. L. & L. SPINELLI 1968: Second successful breeding of cheetahs in a private zoo. Int. Zoo Yearbook 8: 76-78.

FOSTER, J. B. & D. KEARNEY 1967: Nairobi National Park game census, 1966. East Afr. Wildl. J. 5: 112-120.

FOURIE, F. 1972: Excitement over a tame cheetah. Custos 1 (3): 15-17.

FOURIE, F. 1972: Taga, the cheetah. Custos 1 (10): 2-6.

GEE, E. P. 1964: The wildlife of India. Collins, London.

GLASS, B. P. 1965: The mammals of Eastern Ethiopia. Zoologica Africana 1 (1): 177-179.

GRAHAM, A. 1966: East African Wild Life Society Cheetah Survey: Extracts from the report by Wildlife Services. East Afr. Wildl. J. 4: 50-55.

GRAHAM, JANET 1972: George Stubbs, anatomy of an animal painter. Reader's Digest: 64-70.

GRZIMEK, B. & MICHAEL 1960: Serengeti shall not die. Hamish Hamilton, London.

GRZIMEK, B. 1970: Among animals of Africa. Collins, London.

GUGGISBERG, C. A. W. 1970: Man and wildlife. Evans Bros., London.

GÜNTHER, DR 1882: Exhibition of flat skin of a leopard. Proc. Zool. Soc. London: 312.

HANSTRÖM, B. 1949: Cheetahs provide an unusual experience. Afr. Wildl. 3 (3): 203-209.

HARDY, N. G. 1959: The cheetah – fastest animal on earth. Wild Life 1 (3): 27-30.

HARRISON, D. L. 1968: The mammals of Arabia, Vol. II. Ernest Benn, London.

HARTHOORN, A. M. 1973: Review of wildlife capture drugs in common use. In The capture and care of wild animals, ed. E. Young. Human & Rousseau, Cape Town & Pretoria.

HENNIG, R. 1969: Geparden-Vorkommen in Tunesien. Z. Säugetierk. 34 (5): 318-319.

HERDMAN, R. 1972: Captive cheetah reproduction. Zoonooz 45 (10): 4-12.

HEUBLEIN, E. 1968: The cheetah . . . a fast cat. Zoonooz 41 (3): 10-13.

HILDEBRAND, M. 1959: Motions of the running cheetah and horse. J. Mammalogy 40 (4): 481-495.

151

HILDEBRAND, M. 1960: How animals run. Scient. Amer. 202: 148-157.

HILDEBRAND, M. 1961: Further studies on locomotion of the cheetah. J. Mammalogy 42 (1): 84-91.

HIRST, S. M. 1969: Populations in a Transvaal Lowveld Nature Reserve. Zoologica Africana 4 (2): 199-230.

HOLLISTER, N. 1911: The nomenclature of the cheetahs. Proc. Biol. Soc. Wash., 24: 225-226.

HOOGSTRAAL, H. *et al.* 1966-67: The cheetah, *Acinonyx jubatus* Schreber, in Egypt. Bull. Zool. Soc. Egypt 21: 63-68.

HOPWOOD, A. T. 1946: Contributions to the study of some African mammals IV – notes on the interior of the skull in lion, leopard and cheetah. Linc. Soc. Journ.-Zool. Vol. x/i (280): 369-376.

HUNT, D. 1968: The capture of cheetahs. Zoonooz 41 (3): 14-17.

HUNTLEY, B. J. 1972: Preliminary guide to the National Parks and Reserves of Angola. Unpublished.

HUNTLEY, B. J. 1973: Leopard and cheetah survey – notes on the Angolan situation. Unpublished.

HYSLOP, N. ST G. 1955: Feline enteritis in the lynx, the cheetah and other wild felidae. Brit. Vet. J. III (9): 373-377.

JAMES, SIR ARCHIBALD 1962: The puzzle of king cheetahs. The Field May 24: 1018-1019.

JONES, O. G. 1953: Tuberculosis in a cheetah: The use of antibiotics and modern chemotherapeutic agents. The Vet. Record 65 (29): 453.

KEEP, M. E. 1970: Hepatozoonosis of some wild animals in Zululand. The Lammergeyer 12: 70-71.

KEEP, M. E. 1970: Sarcosporidiosis in some wild animals in the Natal and Zululand Game Reserves. The Lammergeyer 12: 66-67.

KELLER, P. W. 1959: Africa's wild glory. Jarrolds, London.

KIRBY, F. V. 1895: In haunts of wild game; a hunter-naturalist's wanderings from Kahlamba to Libombo. Blackwood, London.

KIRKPATRICK, K. M. 1952: A record of the cheetah (*Acinonyx jubatus* Erxleben) in Chitoor District, Madras State. J. Bombay Nat. Hist. Soc. 50 (4): 931-932.

KRUUK, H. & M. TURNER 1967: Comparative notes on predation by lion, leopard, cheetah and wild dog in the Serengeti area, East Africa. J. Mammalia 31 (1): 1-27.

KRUUK, H. 1972: The spotted hyena. University of Chicago Press, Chicago.

KURTÉN, B. 1968: Pleistocene mammals of Europe. Weidenfeld and Nicolson, London.

LAMPREY, H. F. 1964: Estimation of the large mammal densities, biomass and energy exchange in the Tarangire Game Reserve and the Masai Steppe in Tanganyika. East Afr. Wildl. J. 2: 1-46.

LAYARD, E. L. 1861: Record of *Gueparda jubata*. Cat. Mamm. S. Afr. Mus.: 38.

LAYARD, E. L. 1878: Second specimen of *Felis lanea*. Proc. Zool. Soc. London: 655-6.

LEDGER, H. P. 1963: Weights of some East African mammals. East Afr. Wildl. J. 2: 123-124.

LIVINGSTONE, DAVID 1912: Missionary travels and researches in South Africa. Murray, London.

MADDOCK, A. 1971: Animals at peace. Macdonald, London.

MANTON, V. J. A. 1970: Breeding cheetahs at Whipsnade Park. Int. Zoo Yearbook 10: 85-86.

MANTON, V. J. A. 1971: A further report on breeding cheetahs at Whipsnade Park. Int. Zoo Yearbook 11: 125-126.

MANTON, V. J. A. 1974: Birth of a cheetah to a captive-bred mother. Int. Zoo Yearbook 14: 126-129.

MARCHANT, R. A. 1966: Man and beast. Bell, London.

MCLAUGHLIN, R. T. 1970: Aspects of the biology of cheetahs *Acinonyx jubatus* (Schreber) in Nairobi National Park. M.Sc. thesis. University of Nairobi. Unpublished.

MEESTER, J. 1962: King cheetah in northern Transvaal. Afr. Wildl. 16 (1): 81-82.

MEINERTZHAGEN, R. 1938: Some weights and measurements of large mammals. Proc. Zool. Soc. London 108: 433-39.

MILLS, M. G. L. 1973: An unusual case of predation by a leopard in the Kalahari Gemsbok National Park. Custos 2 (8): 39-41.

MILLS, M. G. L. 1974: Carnivores of the Kalahari, Part I. Custos 3 (7): 37-42.

MITCHELL, B. L., J. B. SHENTON & J. C. M. UYS 1965: Predation on large mammals in the Kafue National Park, Zambia. Zoologica Africana 1 (1): 297-318.

MOORE, J. A. 1970: Some notes on the climatic adaptability of large cats in captivity. Int. Zoo Yearbook 10: 144.

MORRIS, R. C. 1935: Distribution of the hunting leopard *(Acinonyx jubatus* Erxl.) in South India. J. Bombay Nat. Hist. Soc. 38 (2): 386-387.

MORRIS, R. C. 1936: Further records of the distribution of the cheetah *(Acinonyx jubatus* Erxl.) in South India. J. Bombay Nat. Hist. Soc. 38 (3): 610.

MORRISON-SCOTT, T. C. S. 1951-1952: Exhibition of photograph of skin of Arabian cheetah. Proc. Zool. Soc. London 121: 201.

MUKHERJEE, AJIT KUMAR (-): Extinct and vanishing birds and mammals of India. Zoological Galleries, Indian Museum, Calcutta.

MURRAY, M., H. CAMPBELL & W. H. F. JARRETT 1964: *Spirocerca lupi* in a cheetah. East Afr. Wildl. J. 2: 164.

MYERS, NORMAN 1972: Salvaging the spotted cat. The Ecologist 2 (3): 8-10.

MYERS, NORMAN 1972: The long African day. Macmillan, New York.

MYERS, NORMAN 1975: The status of the cheetah in Africa south of the Sahara. I.U.C.N. Morges.

NOVIKOV, G. A. 1956: Carnivorous mammals of the fauna of the USSR. Israel Program for Scientific Translations, Jerusalem (1962): 268-271.

ODUM, E. P. 1969: Fundamentals of ecology. Saunders, Philadelphia.

OGNEV, S. I. 1935: Mammals of USSR and adjacent countries: Vol. III Carnivora. Israel Program for Scientific Translations, Jerusalem (1962).

OWEN, RICHARD 1835: On the anatomy of the cheetah, *Felis jubata* Schreb. Trans. Zool. Soc. London 1: 129-137.

PALEN, G. F., & G. V. GODDARD 1966: Catnip and oestrous behaviour in the cat. Animal Behaviour 14 (2-3): 372-77.

PIENAAR, U. DE V. 1963: The large mammals of the Kruger National Park, their distribution and present day status. Koedoe 6: 1-37.

PIENAAR, U. DE V. 1969: Predator-prey relationship amongst the larger mammals of the Kruger National Park. Koedoe 12: 108-176.

PIENAAR, U. DE V., E. LE RICHE & C. S. LE ROUX 1969: The use of drugs in the management and control of large carnivorous mammals. Koedoe 12: 177-183.

POCOCK, R. I. 1916: On some of the cranial and external characters of the hunting leopard or cheetah *(Acinonyx jubatus)*. Ann. & Mag. Nat. Hist. Ser. 8 (18): 419-429.

POCOCK, R. I. 1916: On the hyoidean apparatus of the lion *(F. leo)* and related species of Felidae. Ann. & Mag. Nat. Hist. Ser. 8 (18): 222-229.

POCOCK, R. I. 1927: Description of a new species of cheetah *(Acinonyx)*. Proc. Zool. Soc. London 1: 245-252.

POCOCK, R. I. 1927: The new cheetah from Rhodesia. J. of Soc. for the Preservation of the Fauna of the Empire, Part VII: 17-19.

POCOCK, R. I. 1932: Exhibition of a young cheetah skin. Proc. Zool. Soc. London 2: 814-816.

PORTER, R. N. 1970: An ecological reconnaissance of the Timbavati Private Nature Reserve. Unpublished.

153

POURNELLE, G. H. 1964: The cheetah – associate of aristocracy. Zoonooz 37 (5): 3-7.

RAWLINS, C. G. C. 1972: Cheetahs in captivity. Int. Zoo Yearbook 12: 119-120.
ROBERTS, A. 1951: The mammals of South Africa. Trustees of The Mammals of South Africa Book Fund, Johannesburg, South Africa.
ROOSEVELT, T., & E. HELLER 1914: African game animals. John Murray, London.
ROSENBLATT, D. 1972: Tourist observations. Custos 1 (4): 29-33.
ROSENBLATT, D. 1972: Under the wings of the National Parks Board. Custos 1 (7): 30-37.

SCHALLER, G. B. 1968: Hunting behaviour of the cheetah in the Serengeti National Park, Tanzania. East Afr. Wildl. J. 6: 95-100.
SCHALLER, G. B. 1969: The hunt of the cheetah. Animal Kingdom LXXII (2): 2-8.
SCHALLER, G. B. 1970: This gentle and elegant cat. Natural History LXXIX (6): 31-39.
SCHALLER, G. B. 1972: Are you running with me, Hominid? Predators of the Serengeti, Part 2. Natural History LXXXI (3): 61-68.
SCHALLER, G. B. 1972: The Serengeti lion. University of Chicago Press, Chicago.
SCHALLER, G. B. 1973: Serengeti, a kingdom of predators. Collins, London.
SCHALLER, G. B. 1974: Golden shadows, flying hooves. Collins, London.
SCHALLER, G. B. & G. R. LOWTHER 1969: The relevance of carnivore behaviour to the study of early hominids. Southwest. J. Anthropol. 25: 307-341.
SCHOMBER, H. W. & D. KOCK 1960: The wild life of Tunisia – Part 2. Afr. Wildl. 14 (4): 277-282.
SCLATER, P. L. 1877: Additions to the Society's menagerie. Proc. Zool. Soc. London: 532.
SCLATER, P. L. 1884: Exhibition of skin of *Felis lanea*. Proc. Zool. Soc. London: 476.
SCLATER, W. L. 1900: The mammals of South Africa, Vol. I. Porter, London.
SEAL, U. S., A. W. ERICKSON & J. G. MAYO 1970: Drug immobilisation of the carnivora. Int. Zoo Yearbook 10: 157-170.
SELOUS, F. C. 1908: African nature notes and reminiscences: a facsimile reprint. The Pioneer Head, Salisbury, Rhodesia (1969).
SHAUL, B. D. M. 1962: The composition of the milk of wild animals. Int. Zoo Yearbook 4: 333-42.
SHORTRIDGE, G. C. 1934: The mammals of South West Africa. Heineman, London.
SKEAD, C. J. 1958: Mammals of the Uitenhage and Cradock Districts C.P. in recent times. Koedoe 1: 19-59.
SKELDON, P. C. 1973: Breeding cheetahs at Toledo Zoo. Int. Zoo Yearbook 13: 151-152.
SMITH, R. L. 1966: Ecology and field biology. Harper and Row, New York.
SMITHERS, R. H. N. 1966: The mammals of Rhodesia, Zambia and Malawi. Collins, London.
SMITHERS, R. H. N. 1968: A checklist and atlas of the mammals of Botswana. The Trustees of The National Museums of Rhodesia, Salisbury.
SMITHERS, R. H. N. 1968: Preliminary identification manual for African mammals. No. 25: Carnivora: Felidae. Edited by J. Meester. Smithsonian Institution, United States National Museum, Washington DC.
SMITHERS, R. H. N. 1968: Cat of the pharaohs. Animal Kingdom 61: 16-23.
SMITHERS, R. H. N. 1971: Mammals of Botswana. National Museums of Rhodesia, Salisbury.
SMUTS, G. L., B. R. BRYDEN, V. DE VOS & E. YOUNG 1973: Some practical advantages of CI-581 (Ketamine) for the field immobilisation of larger wild felines, with comparative notes on baboons and impala. The Lammergeyer 18: 1-14.
SPINAGE, C. A. 1968: The book of the giraffe. Collins, London.
STEVENSON-HAMILTON, J. 1929: The lowveld – its wildlife and its people. Cassell, London.
STEVENSON-HAMILTON, J. 1937: South African Eden. Cassell, London.
STEVENSON-HAMILTON, J. 1947: Wildlife in South Africa. Cassell, London.

THOMPSON, R. A. & B. VESTAL 1974: Survey of conditions associated with breeding cheetah in captivity. Oklahoma Zoo Journal 2 (3).

TONG, J. R. 1974: Breeding cheetahs at the Beekse Bergen Safari Park. Int. Zoo Yearbook 14: 129-130.

TRIMEN, R. 1887: Extract from a letter referring to *Felis lanea* of Sclater. Proc. Zool. Soc. XXVII: 397.

TURNBULL-KEMP, PETER 1967: The leopard. Timmins, Cape Town.

ULMER, F. A. 1957: Cheetahs are born. America's First Zoo 9 (3).

VALLAT, CHARLES 1971: Birth of three cheetahs at Montpellier Zoo. Int. Zoo Yearbook 11: 124-125.

VAN DE WERKEN, H. 1967: Preliminary report on cheetahs in zoos and in Africa. Royal Zoological Society, Amsterdam, 1-9.

VAN DE WERKEN, H. 1968: Cheetahs in captivity. Preliminary report on cheetahs in zoos and in Africa. Zool. Garten 35 (3): 156-161.

VANEYSINGA, CAS. R. 1970: A note on keeping cheetahs under winter conditions. Int. Zoo Yearbook 10: 144-146.

VAN INGEN & VAN INGEN 1948: Interesting Shibar trophies: hunting leopard *(A. jubatus)*. J. Bombay Nat. Hist. Soc. 47 (4): 718.

VAN LAWICK-GOODALL, J. 1970: Innocent killers. Collins, London.

VARADAY, D. 1966: Gara Yaka's Domain. Collins, London.

VESEY-FITZGERALD, B. 1967: Enquire within about animals. Pelham Book, London.

VON RICHTER, W. 1969: Survey of the wild animal hide and skin industry. Report to the Government of Botswana, Gaborone.

VON RICHTER, W. 1972: Remarks on present distribution and abundance of some South African carnivores. Jl. Southern Afr. Wildl. Manag. Ass. 2 (1): 9-16.

VON WILHELM, J. H. 1931-32: Gestation of cheetah. J. SWA Sc. Soc., Vol. VI: 71.

WALTHER, F. R. 1969: Flight behaviour and avoidance of predators in Thomson's gazelle. Behaviour XXXIV: 184-221.

WATSON, R. M., A. D. GRAHAM & I. C. S. PARKER 1969: A census of the large mammals of Loliondo controlled area, northern Tanzania. East Afr. Wildl. J. 7: 43-59.

WINTERBOTTOM, J. M. 1971: An introduction to animal ecology in Southern Africa. Maskew Miller, Cape Town.

WRIGHT, B. S. 1960: Predation on big game in East Africa. J. Wildlife Management 24 (1): 1-15.

WYNNE-EDWARDS, V. C. 1962: Animal dispersion in relation to social behaviour. Oliver and Boyd, Edinburgh and London.

YOUNG, E. 1966: The use of tranquilizers, muscle relaxants and anaesthetics as an aid in the management of wild carnivores, 25 case reports. Jl. S. Afr. Vet. Med. Ass. 37: 293-296.

YOUNG, E. 1966: Nutrition of wild South African felines and some viverrids. Afr. Wildl. 20 (4): 293-299.

YOUNG, E. 1967: The hand-rearing of the young of the cat tribes. Afr. Wildl. 21 (1): 21-27.

YOUNG, E. 1972: Cheetahs. Custos 2 (1): 10-12.

YOUNG, E. 1973: The general care and nutrition of wild mammals in captivity. *In* The capture and care of wild animals, ed. E. Young. Human & Rousseau, Cape Town & Pretoria.

YOUNG, E. 1973: Special care and supportive treatment of newly captured wild animals. *In* The capture and care of wild animals, ed. E. Young. Human & Rousseau, Cape Town & Pretoria.

YOUNG, E. 1973: Vaccination and parasite control in wild animals and their general treatment. *In* The capture and care of wild animals, ed. E. Young. Human & Rousseau, Cape Town & Pretoria.

YOUNG, E., F. ZUMPT & I. J. WHYTE 1972: *Notoedres cati* (Hering, 1838) infestation of the cheetah. Prelim. Report. Jl. S. Afr. Vet. Med. Ass. 43: 205.

YOUNG, E., P. J. BURGER & I. J. WHYTE 1972: The use of Dopram-V (doxapram hydrochloride), a potent analeptic, on newly captured wild animals. Veterinary Clinician 11: 11-13.

YOUNG, J. Z. 1962: The life of vertebrates. Oxford University Press, London.

Index

(Except where otherwise indicated, all references are to cheetah)